Seeing Beyond Man-made

By Pamela Ousley

Printed in the United States

Also by Pamela Ousley

<u>Tiaras, Mirrors, & Truth</u>
(available from author)

<u>Sharing Breakfast with Jesus</u>

Author email address: <u>PhotobyPam@aol.com</u>

ISBN 13: 978-0-9815106-5-1

ISBN 10: 0-9815106-5-5

Library of Congress Cataloging-in-Publication Data

Ousley, Pamela – 1956-

Seeing Beyond Man-made – Christian > Glorify God > Photography

1. God 2. Truth 3. Photography 4. Man-made 5. Glorify God 6. Sandals

7. Masts 8. Bible 9. Angel 10. Pulpit 11. Chapel 12. Church

Printed in the United States of America

All inside photographs taken by Pamela Ousley

Back cover photograph of author taken by Lisa Hulsey

Dedicated to all who use photography as a means of artistic expression and all who rely on the Bible as the only way to grow closer to God

GOD'S GLORY MANIFESTED IN PHOTOGRAPHS

Remember how you feel when you walk into a store and immediately see something you desire? Your heart pounds. Your hands twitch. You have found the item for which you have been searching over days, weeks, months, even years. This item was made by man, using a man-made machine. Is this the single, most important item you ever desired? Well, let's look at the man-made objects in our lives. Certainly, we must glorify God because *He* created it all. Every nut, bolt, dowel, piece of fabric, box, metal fastener, *everything* used to make items for our use, God is present in it all because He *created* it all.

Our God can be glorified in so many ways. My love of photography reveals God in everything around me. Human-made objects are made from God-created substances. God is glorified when humankind creates something which shows His handiwork in everything. Even items you would give everything you own to possess.

This book is simply written to show how God can, and *should*, be glorified through our ability to make items from *His* creation. We cannot create without God-provided substances, such as brushes and canvases for paintings, wood for buildings, steel for railroad tracks, metal for cars and trains, stone for steps, paper for books and bags, and plastic for almost everything else we invent. The man-made list of items made from God-created substances is endless. Our gift for invention seems endless.

God gave us phenomenal brains, providing an almost incomprehensible ability to make items for our needs and our desires. We are *still* inventing new items to be used in various ways. Man creates and invents many things to make our lives richer, in our opinion.

Man is God-created. Sometimes I think, *no I know*, we forget this fact. We think we are beings without a Supreme Creator. When we remember God created humans, we are better able to worship Him Who must be worshiped by us – His creation, not the other way around. We can stop worshiping items which are man-made and yet unreliable, imperfect. These man-made items can make our lives simpler, better in many ways. Yet they are man-made from God's substances.

Only God is perfect and eternal. We, His children, are made to live in eternity. But our bodies and lives are not eternal. Even earth as it is today, is not eternal. Only God is unchanging and eternal.

This fact should drop us to our knees in reverent worship and praise to our God.

What I intend is to highlight some of the items I have photographed over the years to glorify God. (Even the camera I use is man-made from God-created substances!) Invented objects serve purposes, of course. But they are not the be all and end all for our existence. Only God is this for us.

We can make many, many objects using our hands, tools, imagination, and various ideas about how to shape and form the objects. He knew He was creating a being with abilities beyond the animals He created. With this God-given knowledge and ability, we were commanded to care for the earth and all He placed there. This is a commandment we must follow with our best intentions.

I am amazed at how much God's talents created within each of us is what motivates us to invent. This book is about how we see our world and how we can manage it to serve our needs and desires. Always remembering to glorify God in our endeavors.

This management can be used for good *and* for bad. We will not discuss the bad ways – products of evil – items may be used. We are speaking of how our human abilities were made to *glorify* God. Not to glorify man or do evil. But, always to glorify our Lord and our Savior.

We were created to worship. We were created to use God-created items to make our lives on earth richer for all who live here. We were created to worship not things or substances, but God Himself. This is what we will discover.

We are created to worship our God. Our King. Our Lord. Our Savior. Worship with music, with song, with hands raised, with our hearts and eyes directed to Him. Worship of objects does not glorify God. As earth's caretakers, we are expected to care for *all* who live here. This is not social justice. Jesus' command to us as Christians is: Love one another.

"And God blessed them. And God said to them, 'Be fruitful and multiply and fill the earth and subdue it, and have dominion over the fish of the sea and over the birds of the heavens and over every living thing that moves on the earth'" (Genesis 1:28). Man is called to be the supreme authority over the earth. He is asked to care for the earth God created, not destroy it. He was created to tame the animals, keeping them in subjection to the rule of the land. In other words, man was created to be God's substitute ruler on earth. Man was not created to undue God's Creation.

Unfortunately, man sinned and did indeed undue the earth God had created for him to live on. Our "rule" was usurped by Satan. No longer rulers, we are in fact ruled by Satan. This does not have to be the way of earth, though. Let's return to our God-glorifying emphasis.

Our praise should not be for the new car or house we just put ourselves in hock to buy. We must be cognizant of those who may not have so much as we have. They might occasionally need our help. Jesus reached out to the people who followed Him. He saw into their hearts and souls, seeing their deepest need – for Him. He healed them and forgave their sins. We can only offer these godly gifts to people through medicine and our human forgiveness. Yet we can feed them, house them, give them a ride, lead them toward the Lord and Savior we know and love. That is the great commission:

> And Jesus came to them and said, "All authority in heaven and on earth has been given to me. Go therefore and make disciples of all nations, baptizing them in the name of the Father and of the Son and of the Holy Spirit, teaching them to observe all that I have commanded you. And behold, I am with you always, to the end of the age."
> (Matthew 28:18-20)

My prayer is this book will encourage those who may take for granted all God has provided for humankind and realize we are called to share our wealth when we can. We can ask Jesus to turn our eyes away from our man-made items and turn them toward Him. See beyond the man-made. We are called to be Christians to our core. Jesus told us to love one another even as we love ourselves. "'And you shall love the Lord your God with all your heart and with all your soul and with all your mind and with all your strength. The second is this: You shall love your neighbor as yourself. There is no other commandment greater than these'" (Mark 12:30-31). We can only accomplish this when we set aside our self-absorption and reach out to our needy world.

Be a serving and giving Christian, using items for God-glorifying purposes. God appreciates *us* appreciating *His* physical gifts to us. And don't forget to thank Him for the brain He has given you to utilize His gifts to create useful items. He gives so we can be better at being humans, living out His commandment to care for His world *and* His people.

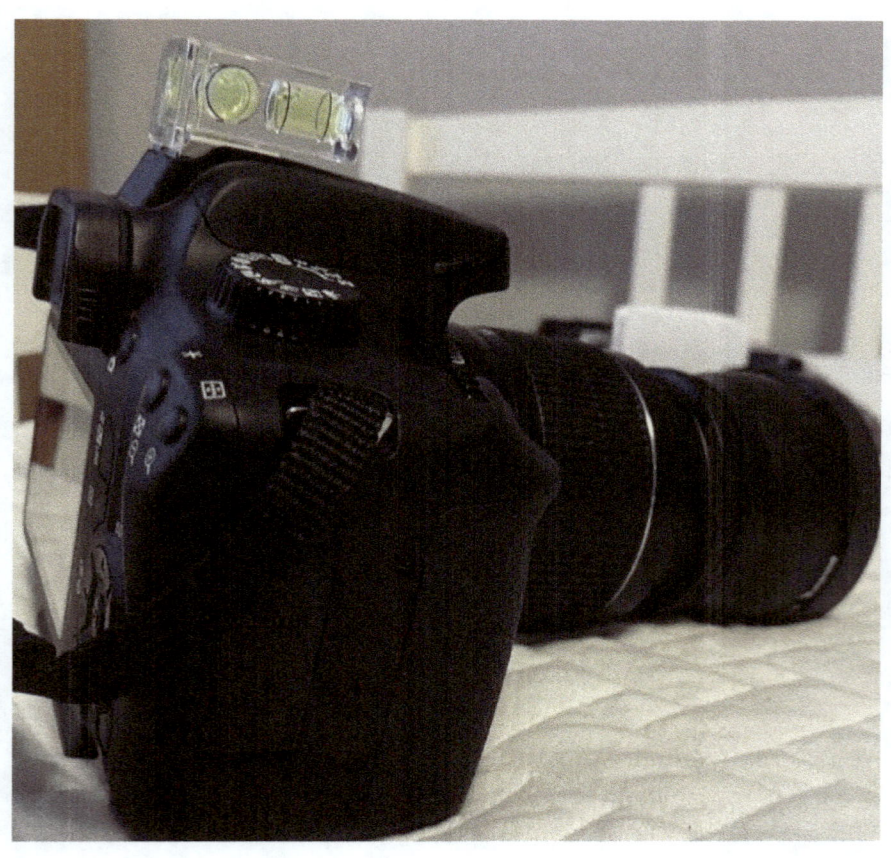

1

The camera had not yet been invented in Jesus' time; however, we now capture items on film or digitally, helping us document them. In ancient times, individuals drew and painted pictures with their limited inventions to adorn their walls. "Then he said to me, 'Son of man, have you seen what the elders of the house of Israel are doing in the dark, each in his room of pictures?'" (Ezekiel 8:12). Each priest was using pictures on the walls for his own interest and enjoyment. Don't we do this with photographs? I have not lost my photography interest. I enjoy creating photographs of man-made items to see and appreciate.

What do pictures on the wall do for us? They remind us of the beauty of our earth. They can brighten our otherwise dreary worlds. Pictures, photographs, and paintings can all be beautiful reminders of God's world. I enjoy going out into nature and photographing the world as I see it. As my mind records and "sees" God's created world, this I attempt to inspire through my photographs.

As mentioned before, we do not live in the world as God created it; however, we are still given enough beauty to deeply appreciate the beauty around us.

Psalm 24
The King of Glory
A Psalm of David

The earth is the LORD's and the fullness thereof,

the world and those who dwell therein,

for he has founded it upon the seas

and established it upon the rivers.

Who shall ascend the hill of the LORD?

And who shall stand in his holy place?

He who has clean hands and a pure heart,

who does not lift up his soul to what is false

and does not swear deceitfully.

He will receive blessings from the LORD

and righteousness from the God of his salvation.

Such is the generation of those who seek him,

who seek the face of the God of Jacob.

Selah

Lift up your heads, O gates!

And be lifted up, O ancient doors,

that the King of glory may come in.

Who is this King of glory?

The LORD, strong and mighty,

the LORD, mighty in battle!

Lift up your heads, O gates!

And lift them up O ancient doors,

that the King of glory may come in.

Who is this King of glory?

The LORD of hosts,

he is the King of glory!

Selah

The Psalm states: lift up your heads, O gates! Horses on each side of this gate lift up their heads and hooves, seeming to be dancing, with no worries in the world. This is how I envision lifting my

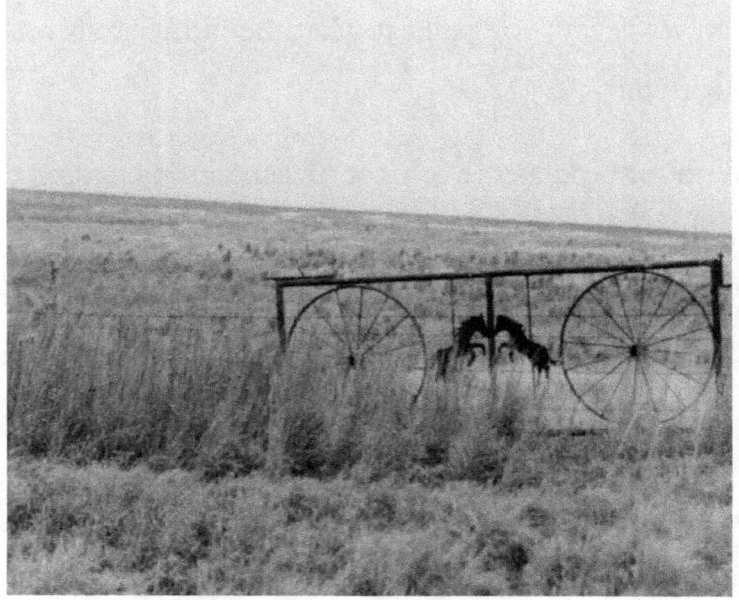

head – with joy and with praise to my God.

A farming tool created by man from God-created materials is a testament to the ingenuity of man. Mankind has created tools from ancient times. God knew this would be a necessity for man to work the land. "Be patient, therefore, brothers, until the coming of the Lord. See how the famer waits for the precious fruit of the earth, being patient about it, until it receives the early and the late rains" (James 5:7).

The farmer's patience should reflect our patience with God in our circumstances. We must seek Him for answers, without rejecting His plan for our lives. All humans are not farmers. Yet we all each what the farmer produces. Whether you eat meat, are vegetarian, or vegan, you still eat what the farmer toils on earth to provide for you.

Without God as the bringer of rain and providing the soil in which the fruit resides, we would have nothing to eat. God provides our every need. Be thankful for the farm machinery built by man to work the soil and provide your food.

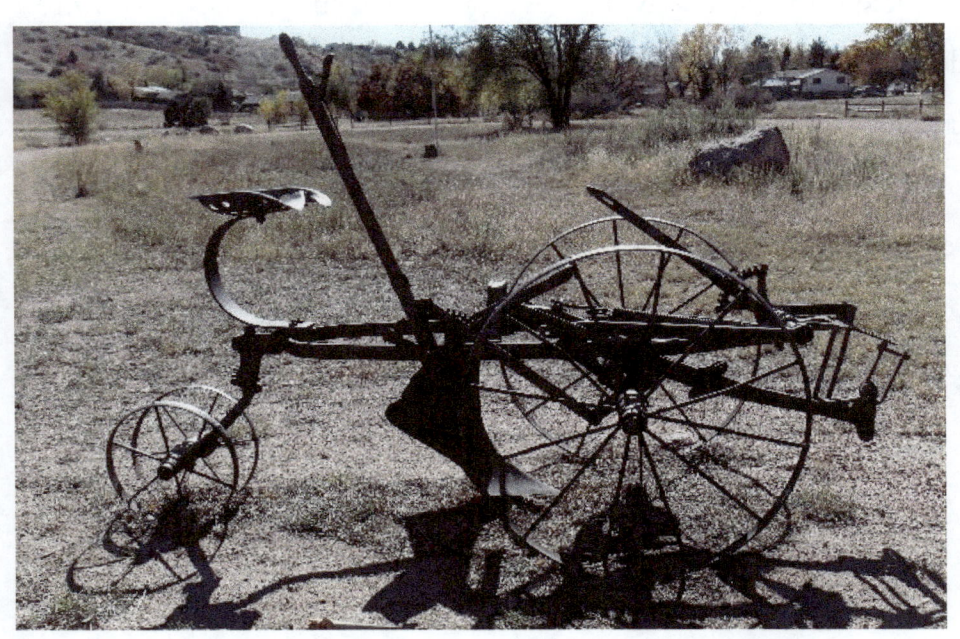

> For if anyone builds on the foundation with gold, silver, precious stones, wood, hay, straw-each one's work will become manifest, for the Day will disclose it, because it will be revealed by fire, and the fire will test what sort of work each one has done. (1 Corinthians 3:12-13)

Men use hay bales in many ways. One might have built hay houses in ancient times. Today; however, hay may still be used. As a fire destroys the house made of hay, our accomplishments can be made of something as tenuous as hay. We rely upon our *work* to sustain us. God expects us to rely on *Him* for our needs. Do you rely on a house made of hay or on the God of the universe? I will put my faith in the God Who created everything before betting on *anything* made by man.

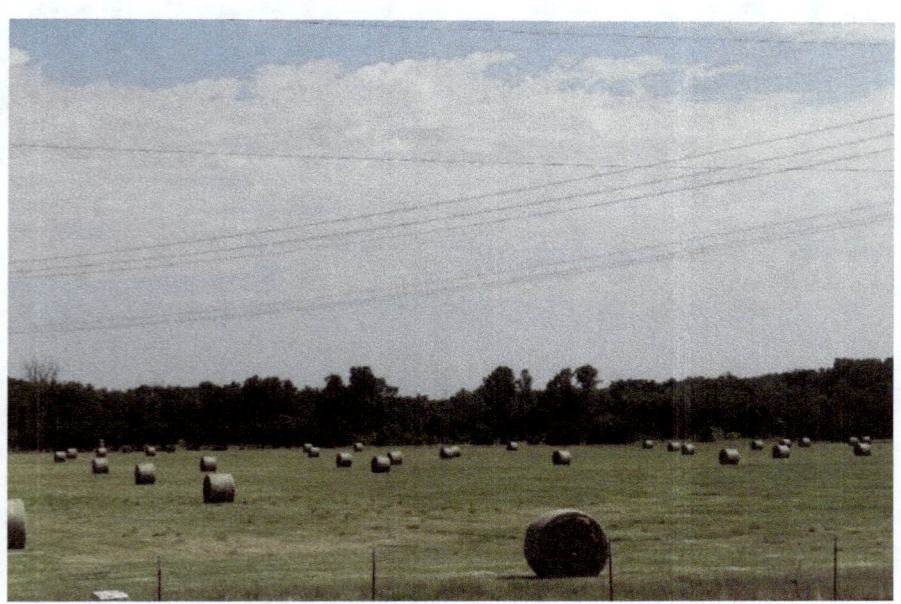

We make fences to provide safe places for livestock to run and eat when brought in by man. We protect gardens and vegetables. Fences keep unwanted predators out who might disturb our livestock or gardens, keeping them safe and controlled via fenced-in areas. "And he began to speak to them in parables. 'A man planted a vineyard and put a fence around it and dug a pit for the winepress and built a tower, and leased it to tenants and went into another country'" (Mark 12:1). A man protected his vineyard.

Sheep are sometimes kept inside a fenced-in area. God fences us in when He is protecting us from danger. He loves us so much He will not allow predators to harm us or tempt us more than we can withstand.

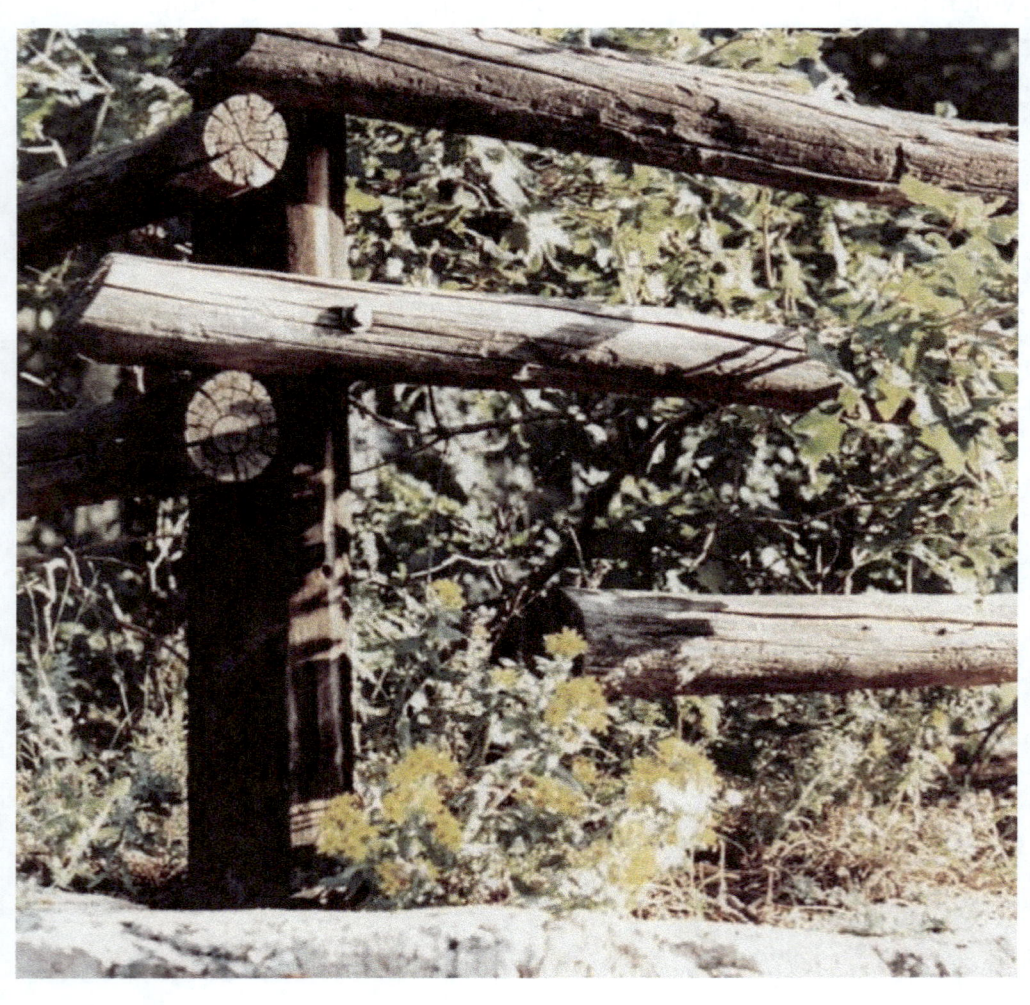

What a beautiful table, waiting and ready for individuals to utilize its steady chairs and table legs to hold them and their anticipated food. Jesus, when dining at a table as a guest, surprised His host:

> One of the Pharisees asked him to eat with him, and he went into the Pharisee's house and took his place at the table. And behold, a woman of the city, who was a sinner, when she learned that he was reclining at table in the Pharisee's house, brought an alabaster flask of ointment, and standing behind him at his feet, weeping, she began to wet his feet with her tears and wiped them with the hair of her head and kissed his feet and anointed them with ointment. (Luke 7:36-38)

Jesus told the Pharisee a parable, then turned His attention to the woman. He rebuked the Pharisee for being negligent in caring for Him as He joined him at this meal. Jesus turned directly to the woman and said, "'Your sins are forgiven. … Your faith has saved you; go in peace'" (Luke 7:48b, 50b).

Jesus wanted the guests and the Pharisee to understand He had authority to forgive sin. This is no small evidence of Jesus' authority as God. He interrupted His meal to address the woman *and* give her the life-giving forgiveness of sin.

He saw her. He heard her. He recognized her need for forgiveness. He responded with His lovingkindness. This response is what we request when we go to Jesus with our prayers. God forgave us. We should accept His forgiveness. We must also offer our forgiveness to those who may hurt or disappoint us on this God-created earth. This is a commandment from God.

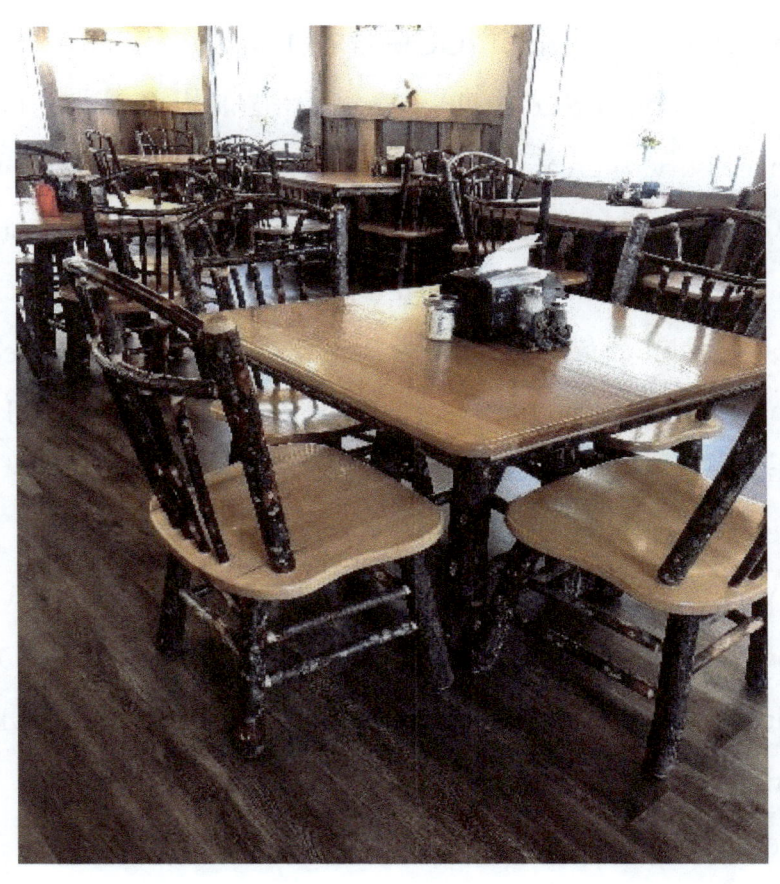

"And Melchizedek king of Salem brought out bread and wine. (He was priest of God Most High.) And he blessed him and said, 'Blessed be Abram by God Most high, Possessor of heaven and earth; and blessed be God Most High, who has delivered your enemies from your hand!'" (Genesis 14:18-19).

Jesus is our bread of life. We are unable to provide the items necessary to create our life-giving bread, given to us by Jesus. God must provide both the substances required for our physical bread and the bread of life through His Son, Jesus Christ. This is the link between what God provides for our every need and what we do with what He provides. We eat of the bread on earth, made by man. We spiritually take of the Bread of Life provided by His Son, Jesus Christ.

What do you think of when you contemplate God's world and how we can use His materials to create useful objects? Do you think about these things? Do you think about ways in which you can glorify God when you see objects made by humans because of talent and ability provided by God?

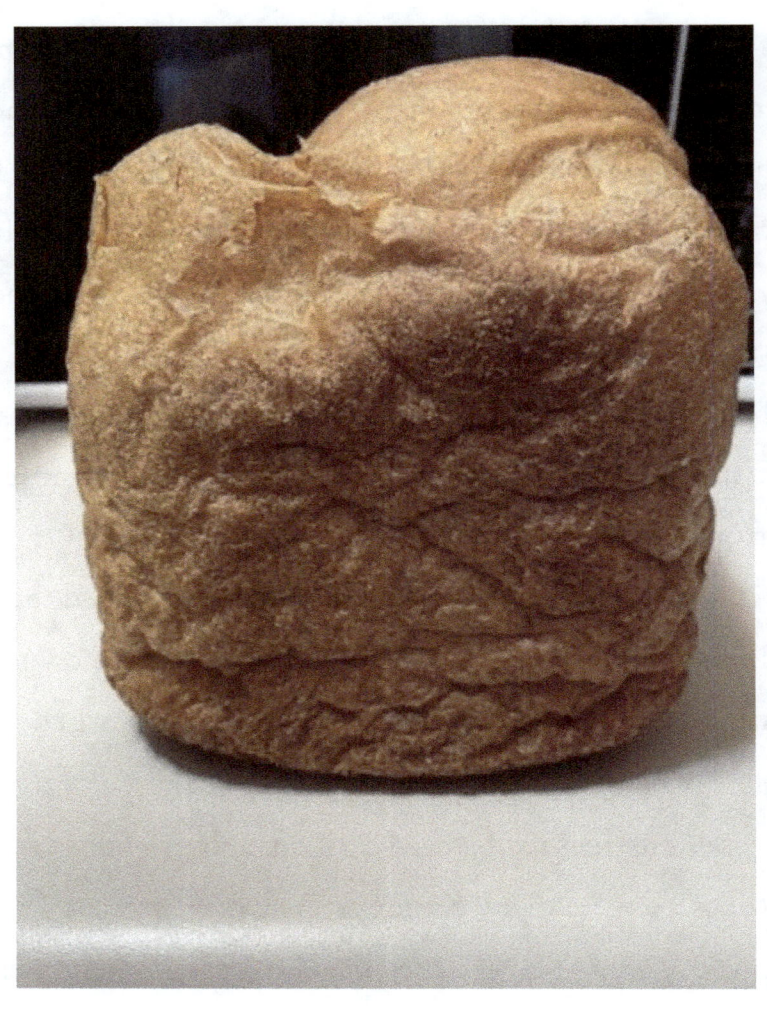

One of the great Old Testament stories tells of the prostitute, Rahab, rescuing two men sent by Joshua to scout out Jericho in anticipation of entering the land to conquer it. The two men entered the city and lodged with Rahab. Men inside the town discovered the strangers were there. They went to Rahab's house to capture the two men. Rahab, however, had another idea. The men escaped: "Then she let them down by a rope through the window, for her house was built into the city wall, so that she lived in the wall" (Joshua 2:15).

The rope below is not the rope Rahab used, but we use rope for all types of things, don't we? Sometimes they can rescue people from places like wells in which they have fallen. Or provide a way to escape a burning building. God created the material for ropes to be made to use as rescue items in dangerous situations. Holding onto the rope God extends to us when we need help is what God intends. Pray for Him to rescue you. Rescue ropes are man-made, used by man, and provided by God.

Ropes come in many contexts. They may appear as a bridge for us to use to cross a river. They may be seen as a hand held out to us to help us out of a predicament. A rope can look like a gift to get us from one place to another.

Ropes, in every way, are gifts, providing assistance. The rope Rahab used saved the two men from capture and the thwarting of God's plan for Israel. That rope was indeed important for our future, also.

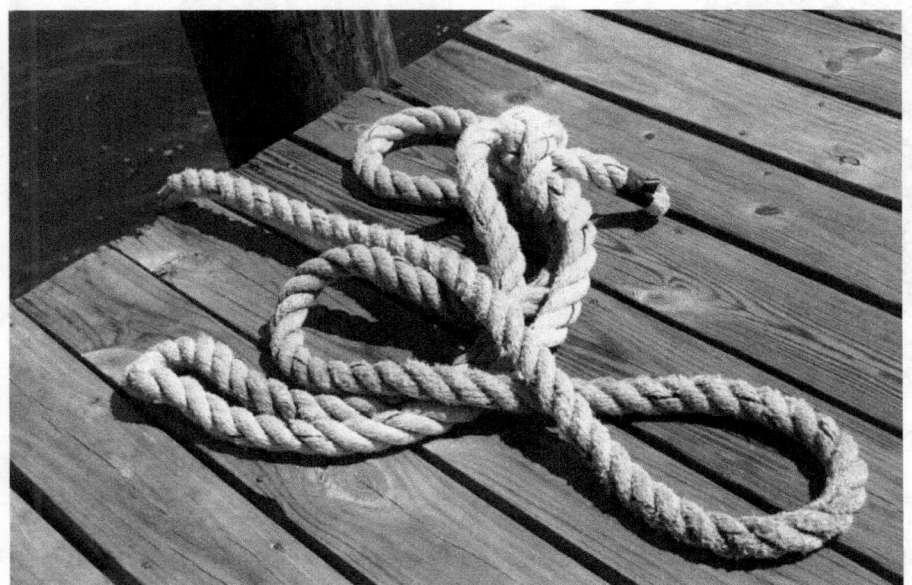

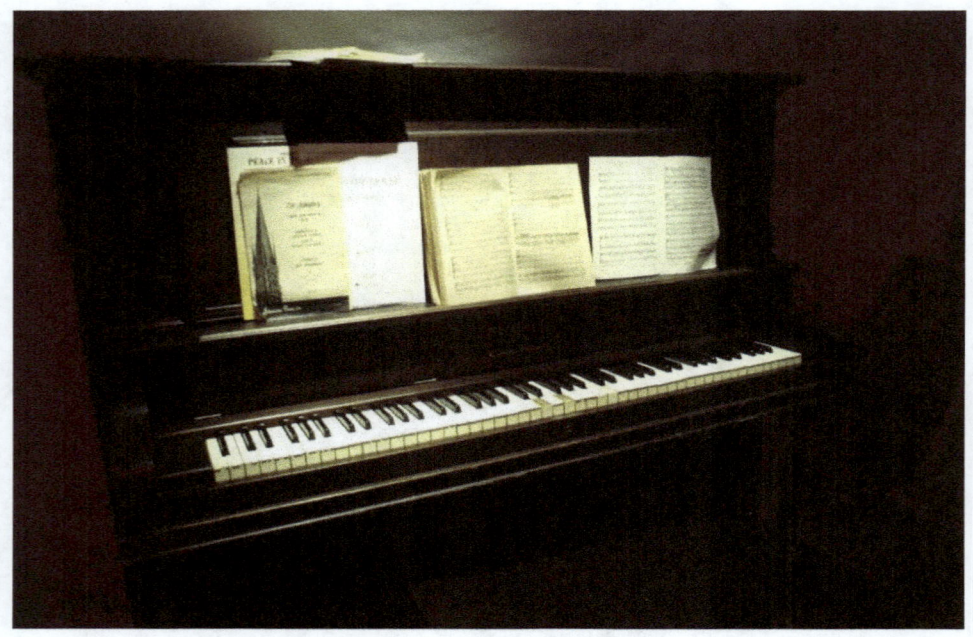

Music was used by David to calm King Saul. "And whenever the harmful spirit from God was upon Saul, David took the lyre and played it with his hand. So Saul was refreshed and was well, and the harmful spirit departed from him" (1 Samuel 16:23).

How often has Christian music soothed your aching, weary soul? It can calm me immediately. Music is used to praise our Lord. We sing praise music in our churches. We are lifted up to glorify God in our praise songs.

When you hear a stirring rendition of a hymn such as "How Great Thou Art" are you not lifted to your feet in reverent worship? I am. The words surely evidence how great our God is. What better way to glorify Him than by singing of His *greatness*.

2

"I write these things to you who believe in the name of the Son of God, that you may know that you have eternal life" (1 John 5:13). John used writing to convey his heart-felt knowledge about the God of the universe and Jesus Christ, His Son. He encouraged readers, providing assurance of their eternal life through Jesus Christ.

We now primarily use computer keyboards to document our written words. Man invented the typewriter to provide an easier way than writing by hand. Scribes faithfully copied word for word our Holy Bible, giving us the first written Word of God for our edification. What a wonderful gift from God – to use words to convey our deepest emotions and thoughts. What a fantastic gift of God – giving us the Holy Bible to document *His* Word.

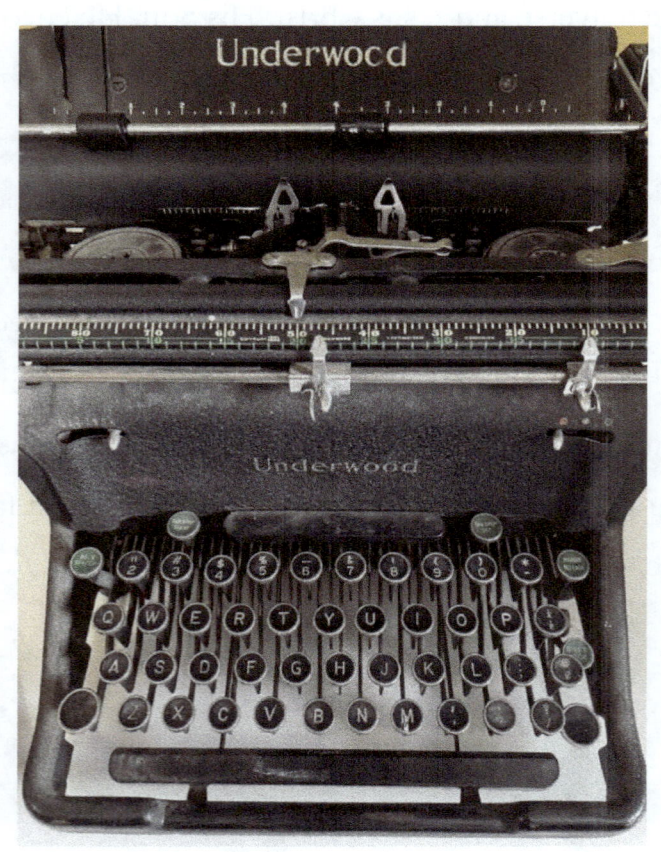

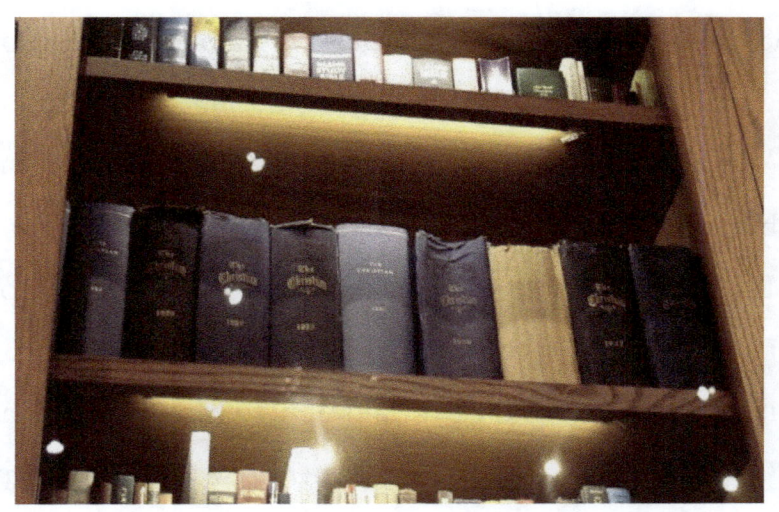

Billy Graham's library is filled with God-glorifying books containing inspired words of the Holy Spirit. They are worth reading every word. John made an interesting comment: "Now there are also many other things that Jesus did. Were every one of them to be written, I suppose that the world itself could not contain the books that would be written" (John 21:25). Apparently, the Holy Bible contains merely a few of the acts done and the Words spoken by Jesus while He was on earth. We have enough difficulty reading and understanding the Bible in its entirety. How could we understand and grasp *all* the Words and actions of our Lord? Theologians have written books for centuries based on understanding Jesus' actions and Words. To think about the whole world being filled with books of what Jesus did and said is incomprehensible. We have, apparently, not even scratched the *surface* of what Jesus accomplished on earth.

I found a Bible torn apart and resting on a table. The map page opened for all to see showed the region during Jesus' time on earth. Was He telling us to remember His holy land? The page of the Bible which can be seen contains a familiar verse: "'For I know the plans I have for you, declares the LORD, plans for wholeness and not for evil, to give you a future and a hope. Then you will call upon me and come and pray to me, and I will hear you'" (Jeremiah 29:11-12). What a *perfect* verse for God to give us in this torn Bible.

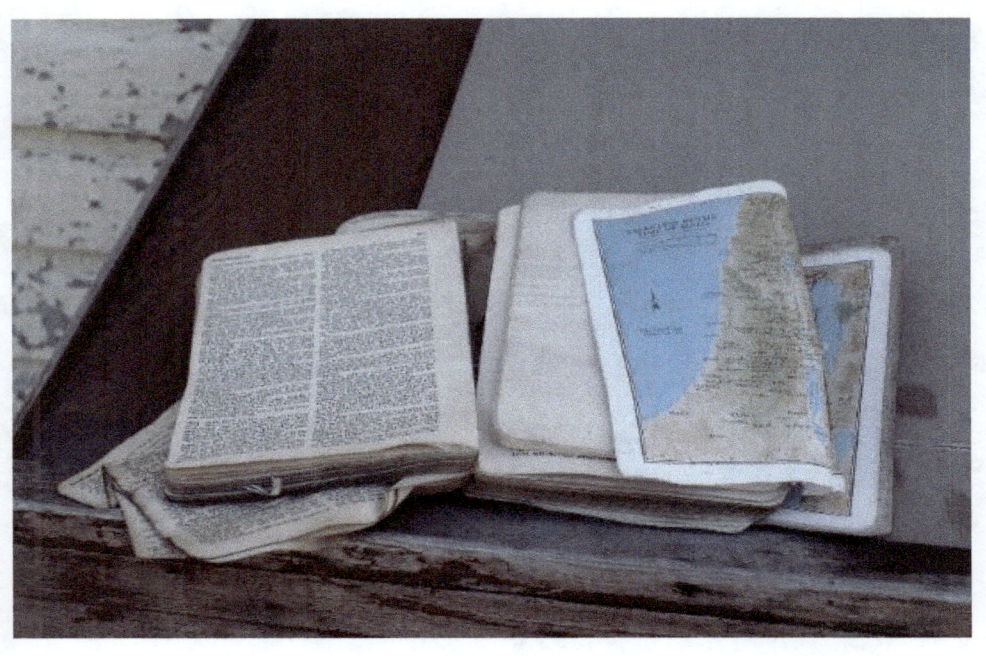

3

Hebrews speaks of Jesus as a high priest more than once.

> We have this as a sure and *steadfast anchor of the soul*, a hope that enters into the inner place behind the curtain, where Jesus has gone as a forerunner on our behalf, having become a high priest forever after the order of Melchizedek. (Hebrews 6:19-20 Emphasis mine)

We use anchors to keep boats from straying. God's Word tells us how He is *our anchor of the soul*. He keeps our hearts from straying. We are prone to wander, as a well-known hymn says. We can only go so far as God allows. This encouraging Truth is good to know, especially in times of confusion or trouble.

Jesus is our high priest. Our sure anchor for the soul. My Savior is always interceding on my behalf. I cannot make it through life without His steady anchor of my soul, keeping me safely in one spiritual place as He works within my confused and often frightening life circumstances.

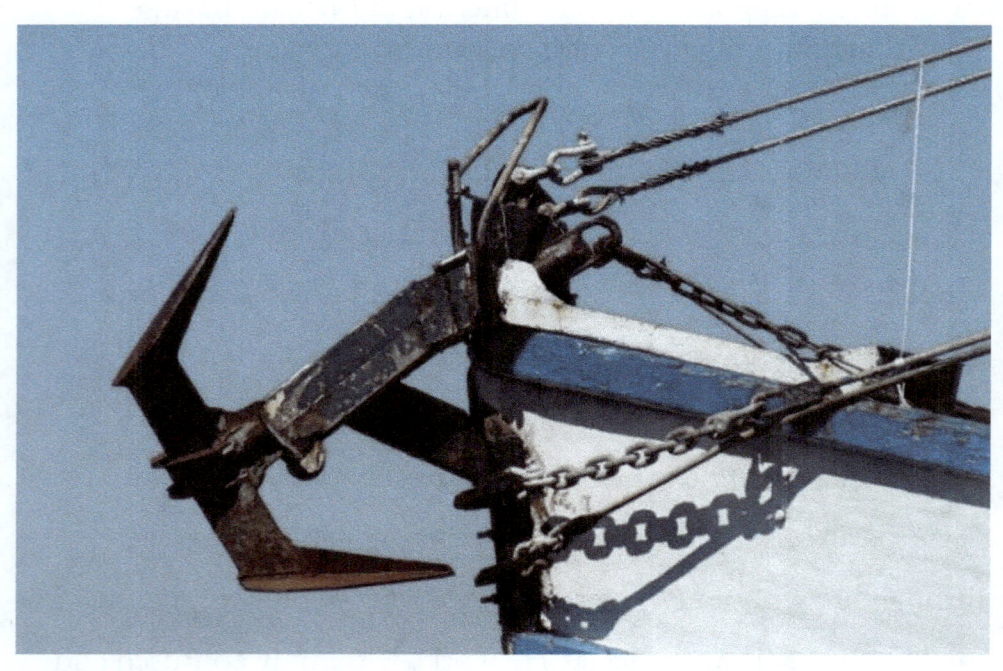

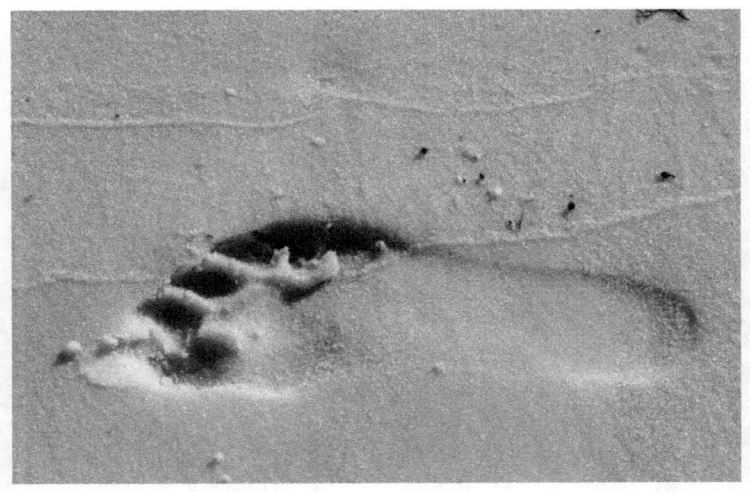 This is not Jesus' footprint. Yet it is *someone's* footprint in the sand, much like Jesus' would have appeared as He walked about on His ministry journey. Can't you just see Jesus, walking on the sand at the Sea of Galilee?

Men make imprints of their feet in the sand even as Jesus was the perfect image of God for us on earth. "He is the radiance of the glory of God and the exact imprint of his nature, and he upholds the universe by the word of his power" (Hebrews 1:3a). Jesus exactly reveals the Father to us, the same way our footprint in the sand exactly reveals the imprint of our foot. This image is a perfect example of how Jesus is the exact imprint of God, the Father. If we look at Jesus, we can't help but envision the Lord our God, our Father. Hebrews tells us how we can see God without setting our eyes upon Him. Look to Jesus. See the Father.

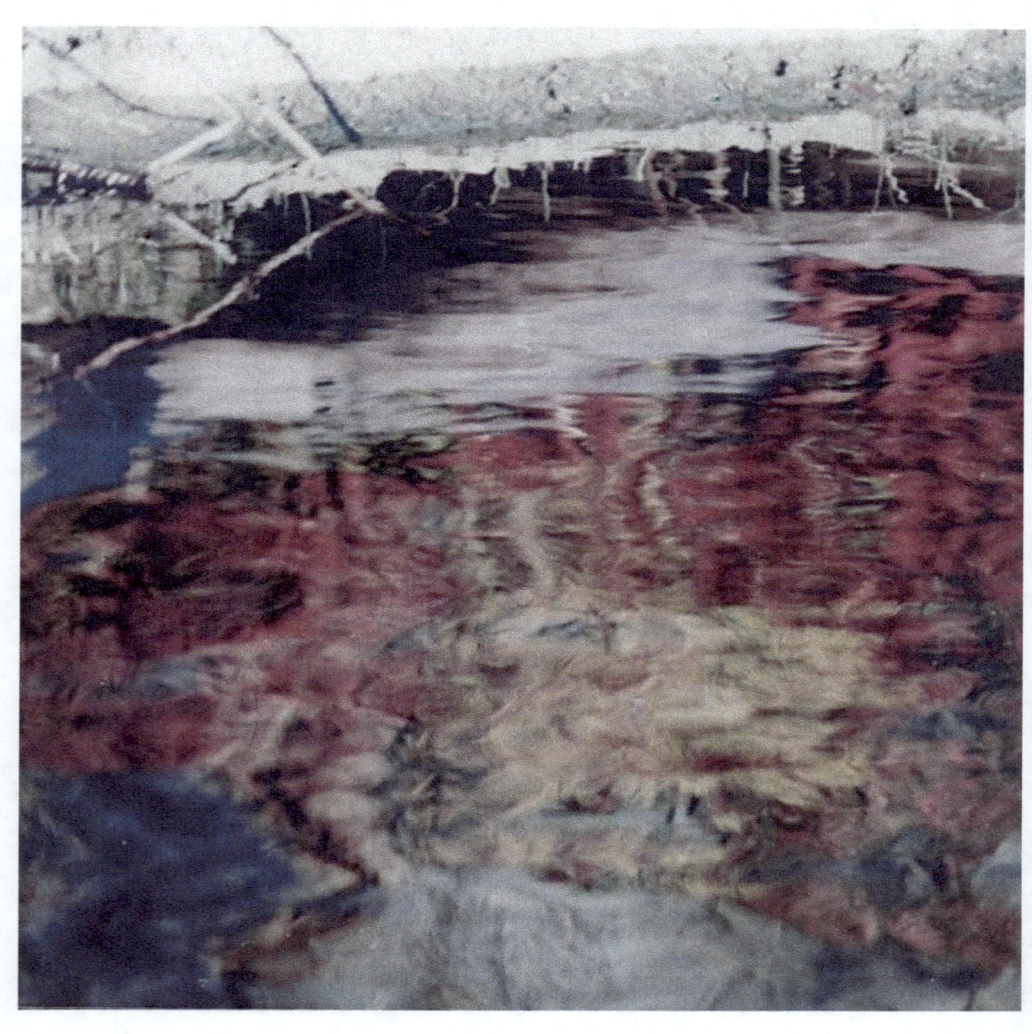

"As in water face reflects face, so the heart of man reflects the man" (Proverbs 27:19). Glass mirrors were invented by Romans around the third century. Men could previously see their reflection in water such as lakes or rivers. This reflection could not, however, be so distinct as a man-made mirror.

1 Corinthians 13:12 states: "For now we see in a mirror dimly, but then face to face. Now I know in part, but then I shall know fully, even as I have been fully known."

When Christians graduate to heaven they will recognize being fully known by God and they will know fully. This Truth is *awesome* in its magnificence. See your reflection in the water. Ponder your heart's reflection. Think deeply about being known, fully, by the Creator of the universe.

How would we prepare our God-given food without the stove? People used other forms of cooking and baking prior to this invention. Old Testament individuals prepared grain offerings to the Lord:

> And if your offering is a grain offering baked on a griddle, it shall be of fine flour unleavened, mixed with oil. You shall break it in pieces and pour oil on it; it is a grain offering. And if your grain offering is a grain offering cooked in a pan, it shall be made of fine flour with oil. And you shall bring the grain offering that is made of these things to the Lord, and when it is presented to the priest, he shall bring it to the altar. (Leviticus 2:5-8)

We might be hard pressed to create some of the meals we eat now without this man-made invention.

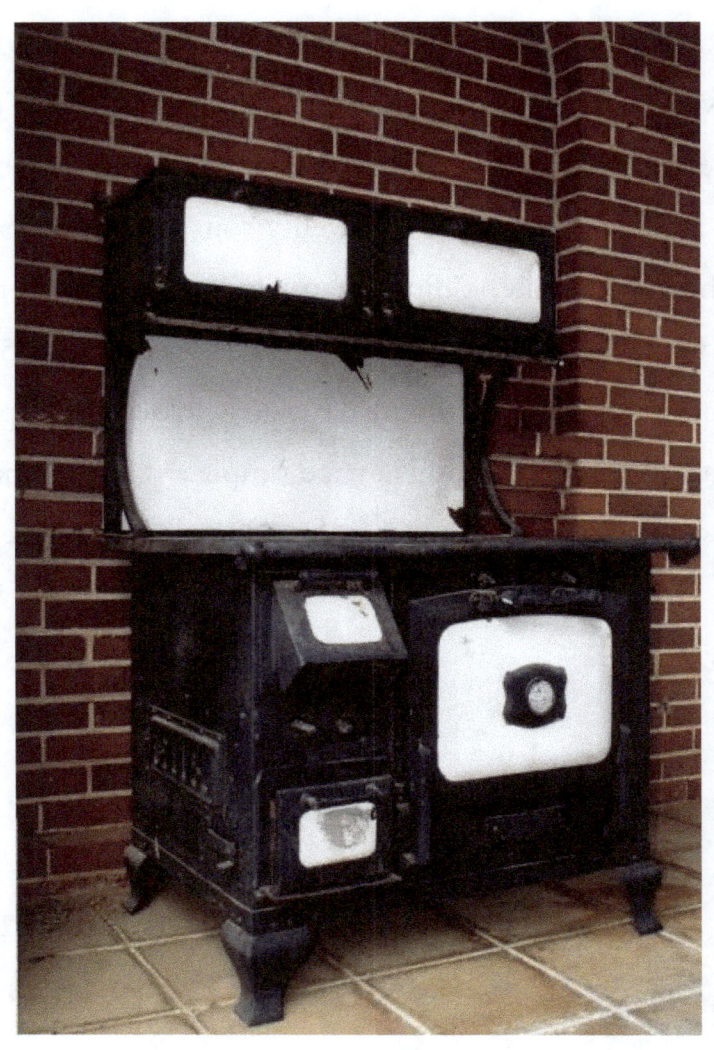

How about what holds your food, keeping it contained while you eat? Bowls are an ingenious way to hold our meals. What about other uses for bowls, though? "And when he had taken the scroll, the four living creatures and the twenty-four elders fell down before the Lamb, each holding a harp, and golden bowls full of incense, which are the prayers of the saints" (Revelation 5:8). Think about our *prayers* being held inside a golden bowl, presented to the Lamb of God. Isn't this image simply a precious thought to hold onto? Our prayers, no matter how large or small, are all held in Jesus' Hands inside a golden bowl, to be answered as His Father wills.

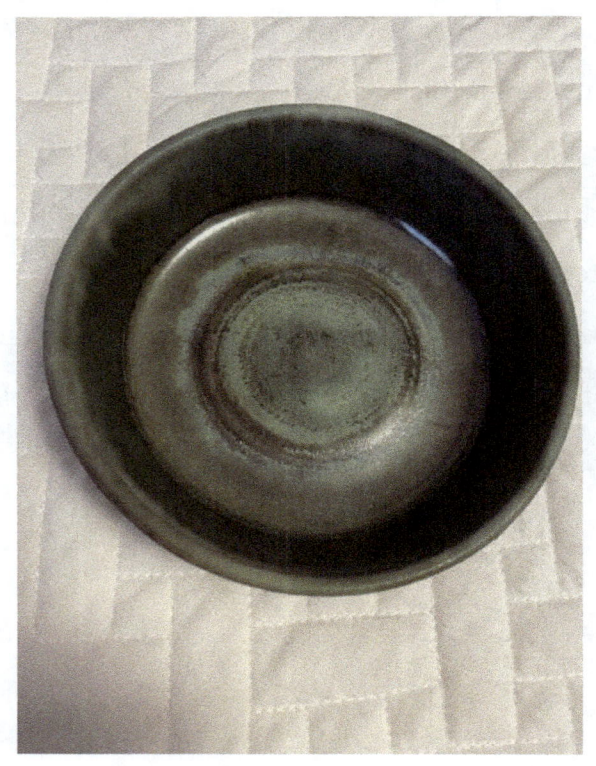

Baskets are utilized to hold man-made items. The baskets themselves are man-made. Some baskets are quite ornate and intricately made. I enjoy baskets – to hold, to place items inside, to be a place for flowers or food items.

Baskets are meant to be used to safely hold our God-given items. "'Then the priest shall take the basket from your hand and set it down before the altar of the LORD your God'" (Deuteronomy 26:4). Baskets were used to hold the offerings placed at the altar of our Lord. God accepted the offerings placed inside the man-made basket as a holy offering to Him. Setting our offerings before the altar makes them a holy offering. They are not holy items, but holy offerings presented inside a man-made item. Holy offerings is what God desires from us – *His* creation.

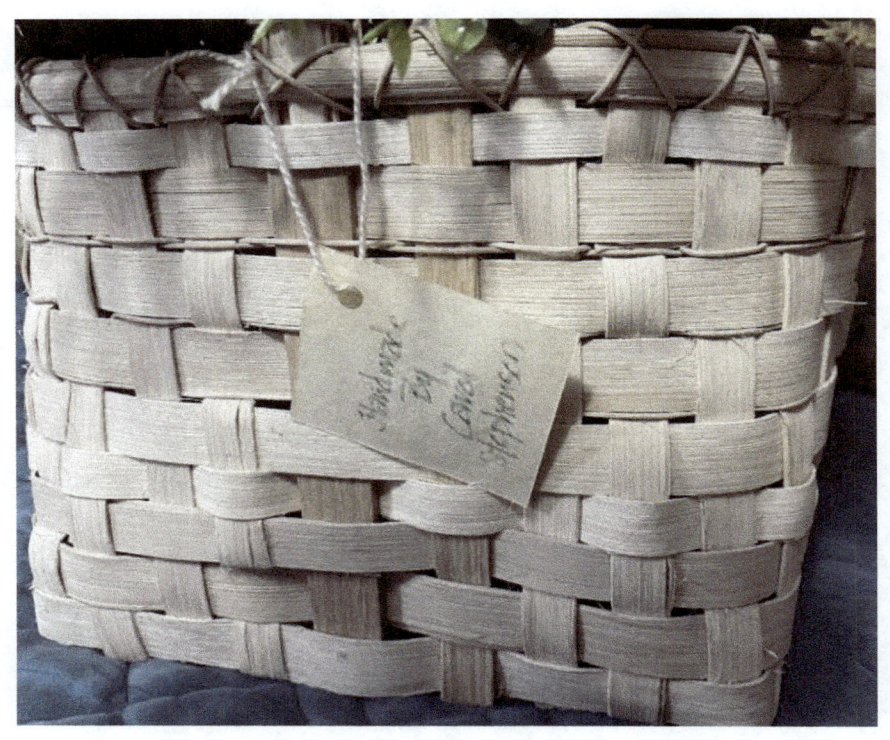

What about stone steps created to make our footing surer while climbing steep hills? "'My foot has held fast to his steps; I have kept his way and have not turned aside'" (Job 23:11).

4

Are your feet steadier as you climb a hill using steps? Or do you find yourself turning aside if the hill becomes seemingly too steep? We all face temptations in life. As you climb your hill(s), use the steps man has provided for you. Use also the steps provided by God to keep your feet steady and not turning aside toward temptation. He loves you so much He doesn't want your feet to slip, causing you to fall away from Him. He provides solid, sure steps for you to use as your guide and your steadiness, even in the worst times.

> Therefore let anyone who thinks that he stands take heed lest he fall. No temptation has overtaken you that is not common to man. God is faithful, and he will not let you be tempted beyond your ability, but with the temptation he will provide the way of escape, that you may be able to endure it. (1 Corinthians 10:13)

I know the temptations I have endured and how I, by myself, handled them poorly. Since my return to the God of Creation, I am now able to withstand temptation because of His sure steps provided for me to stay walking steadily upon. I thank God for His steps and His steady Hand holding mine.

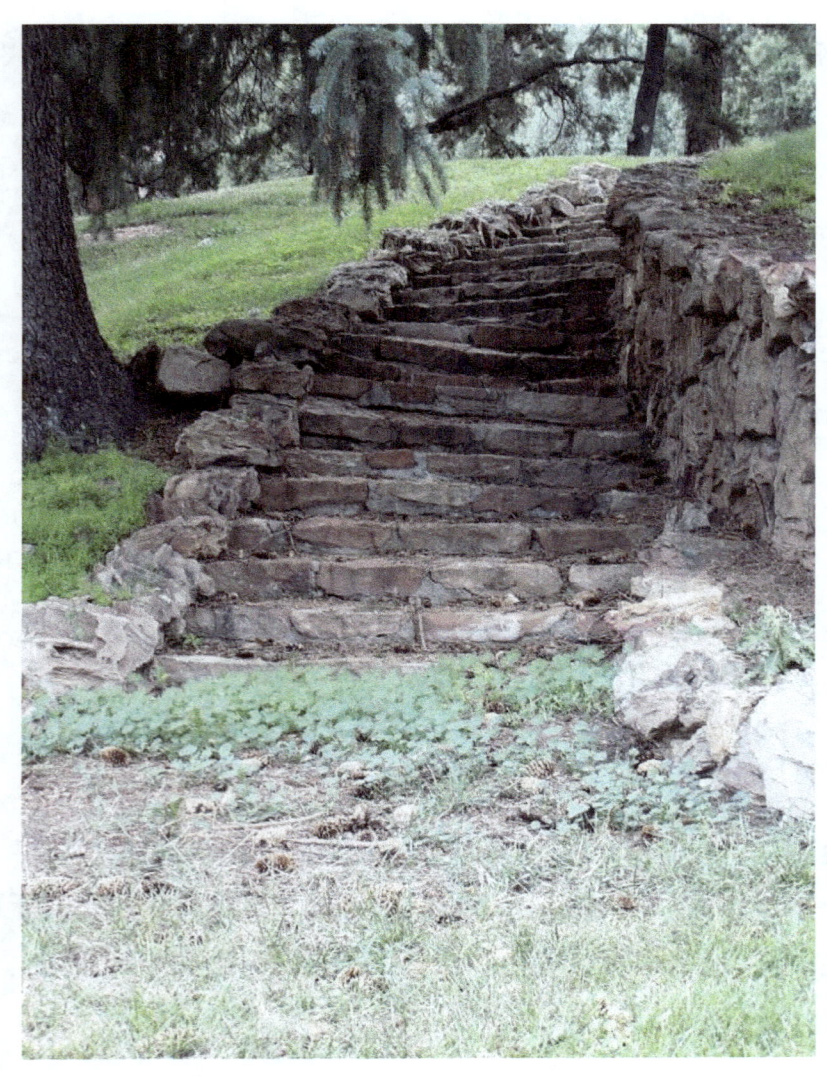

When I look around, I am simply amazed at the myriads of things available for us to take and use for our needs and our wants. It is astonishing how much we are given and how much we make use of these objects and the necessary building materials.

"'The wind blows where it wishes, and you hear its sound, but you do not know where it comes from or where it goes. So it is with everyone who is born of the Spirit'" (John 3:8). God created

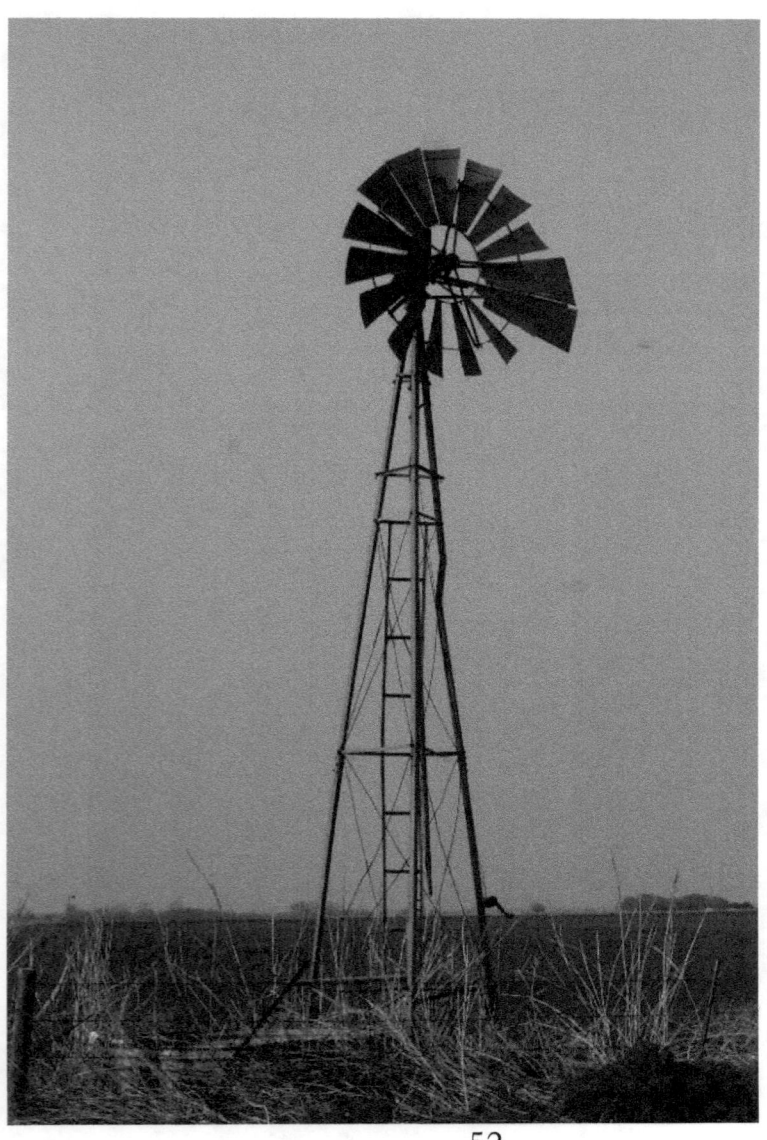

the wind. We have learned how to harness the wind to our benefit.

We can't explain from where it originates nor where it goes when it passes by. Yet we know the importance of wind. And we know the importance of the Holy Spirit. Those born of the Spirit are children of God. He is sovereign over their lives.

I often think the wind is almost sovereign over my *hair* when it blows. Yet I am reminded every time the wind does blow, it is God-provided evidence of *His* sovereignty.

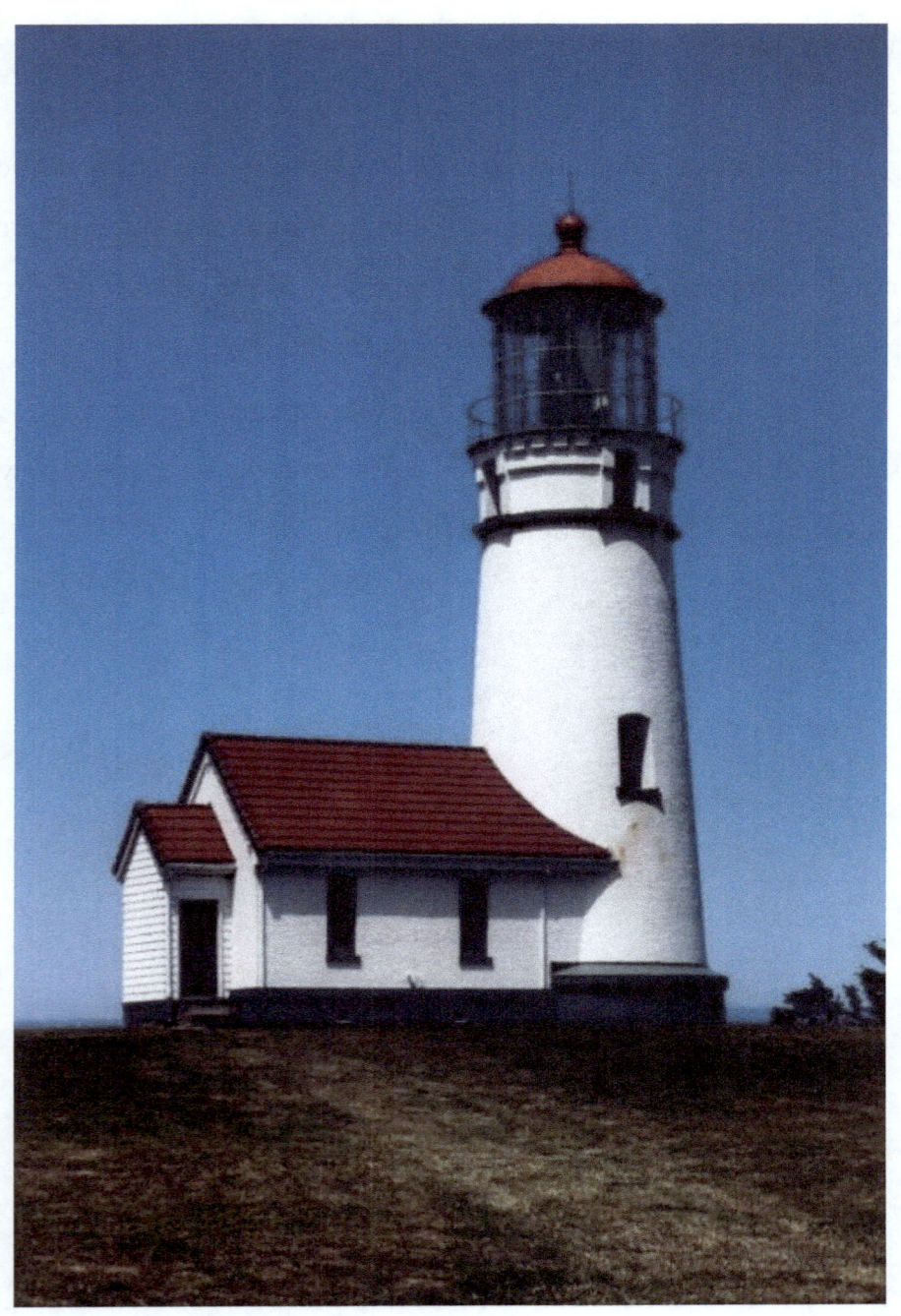

54

Light was created by God on His first day of Creation. "And God said, 'Let there be light,' and there was light" (Genesis 1:3). Man uses light certainly as protection from dark. A lighthouse stands guard over waters used by boats and ships. The captains know where the shore is by steering by the light from the lighthouse. Our Light comes from a Person, the Person of Jesus Christ. "'As long as I am in the world, I am the light of the world'" (John 9:5). Jesus said this to His Disciples as they passed by a blind man.

What an awesome way for Him to show them how light is essential for us to "see" in the dark. We are surrounded by darkness in this life. God provides our light through His Son - Jesus Christ.

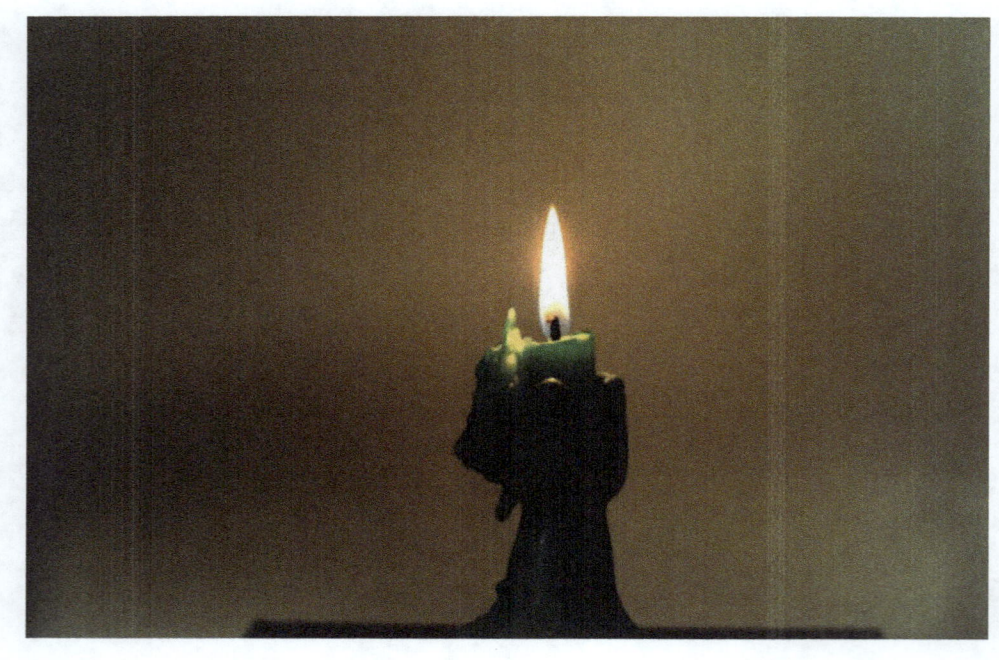

Man utilizes light with lit candles. Before electricity was discovered by man, candles often lit the way for individuals to walk in the dark, seeing their way to their destinations. Without light, we would be limited to traveling well only during the daylight hours. Dark would be a frightening part of life, with no way to navigate it in this world.

Jesus' "light" is what we must seek in the darkness, to see our way and to reach out to Him in our deepest needs. "At the same time, it is a new commandment that I am writing to you, which is true in him and in you, because the darkness is passing away and the true light is already shining" (1 John 2:8).

"'And there shall be no night there, and they need no candle, neither light of the Sun: for the Lord God giveth them light, and they shall reign for evermore'" (Revelation 22:5, The 1599 Geneva Bible). Candles, indeed, still provide light in the darkness. They are used less frequently today. Yet people make them available in many colors, sizes, shapes, and scents.

"And we have the prophetic word more fully confirmed, to which you will do well to pay attention as to a lamp shining in a dark place, until the day dawns and the morning star rises in your hearts" (2 Peter 1:19). God's Word is a lamp for our feet: "Your word is a lamp to my feet and a light to my path" (Psalm 119:105).

His Word lights our physical paths *and* our spiritual journeys. We can walk with confidence knowing His Word lights our way. Jesus overcame the darkness of this world. We are free to travel in God's light, sure of our steps and our lighted way.

I know I appreciate the lamps man has provided for my walks at night. When the street is lighted well enough to keep me from stumbling and/or falling, I think of the lights provided by men to keep us safe and on the right road. Just as God keeps us on the correct *spiritual* paths.

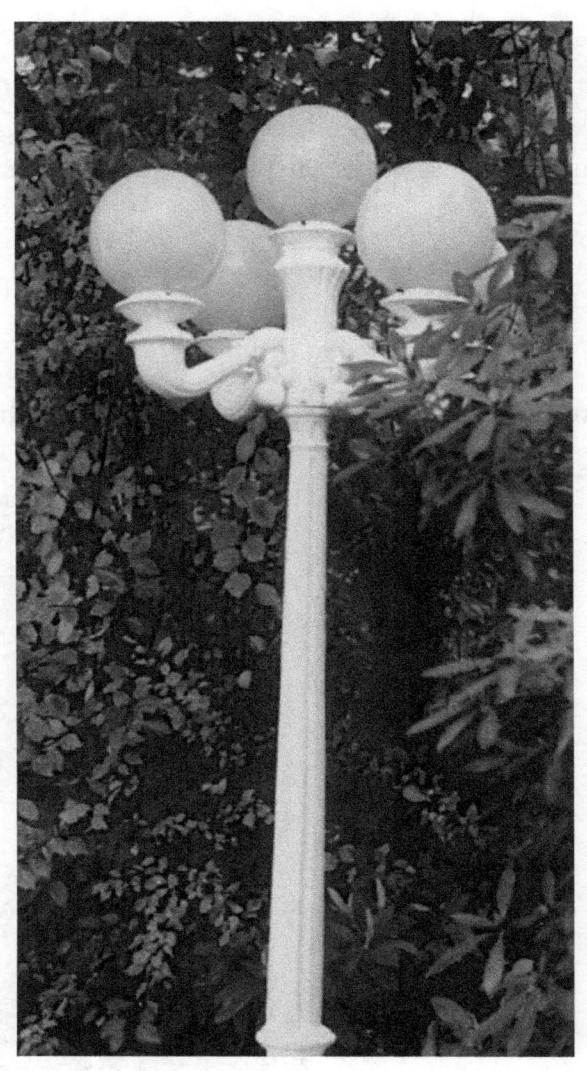

Man can create towers that reach high into the sky. The Bible speaks of the man-made tower of Babel.

> Then they said, 'Come, let us build ourselves a city and a tower with its top in the heavens, and let us make a name for ourselves, lest we be dispersed over the face of the whole earth. (Genesis 11:4)

When individuals began building the Tower of Babel, God put a stop to their endeavor. He did exactly as they feared He would. He, in fact, dispersed them over the face of the earth.

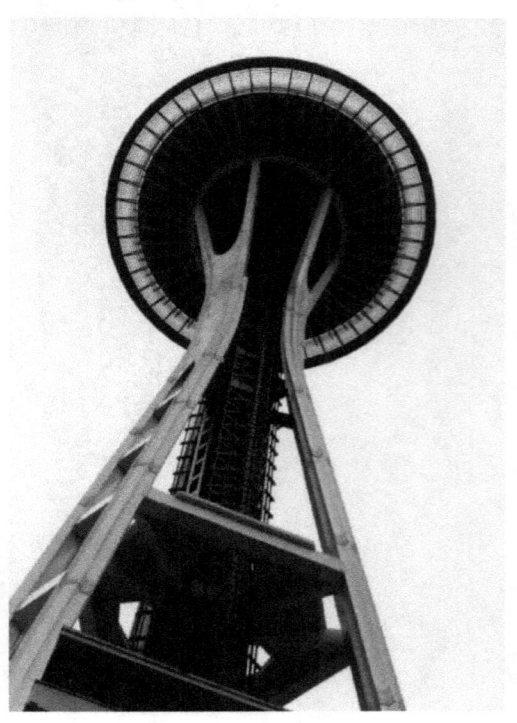

What does this say about people attempting to build beyond God's wishes? I believe He will not be successfully *opposed* by the people He created.

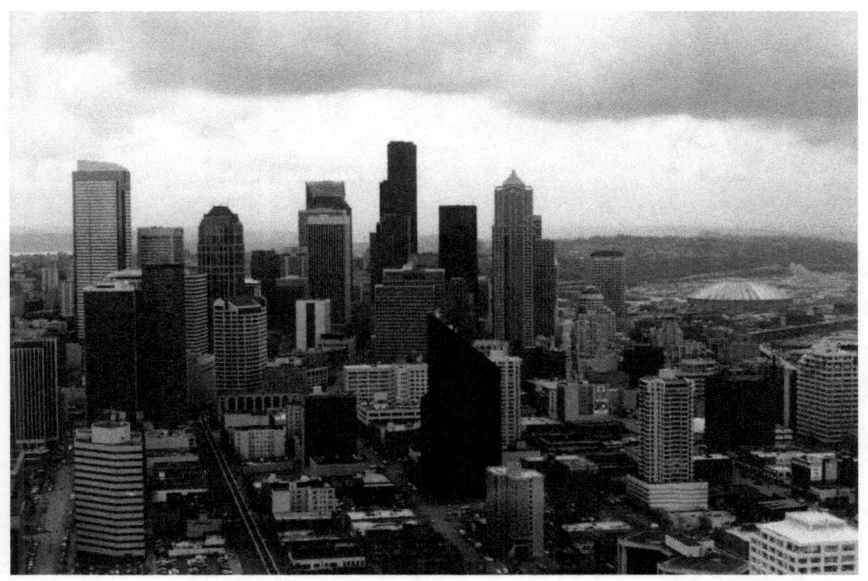

Cities grow larger every day, much to God's chagrin, I believe. We rely on cities for people to live and work. We do not physically and emotionally provide for everyone who lives in these cities, though. Our emphasis is upon making more, doing more, accomplishing more, all *without* relying on God as our Creator. Revelation 16:19 speaks of the cities of the nations falling. Do we recognize civilizations which have not survived? We remember them, trying to keep their histories alive. God wants these cities to glorify Him. We are not doing His will by building more and more, without any thought to how this may affect humans residing there.

On the other hand, birds of the air rely upon man to sometimes provide small dwellings for them to build their nests in and care for their young:

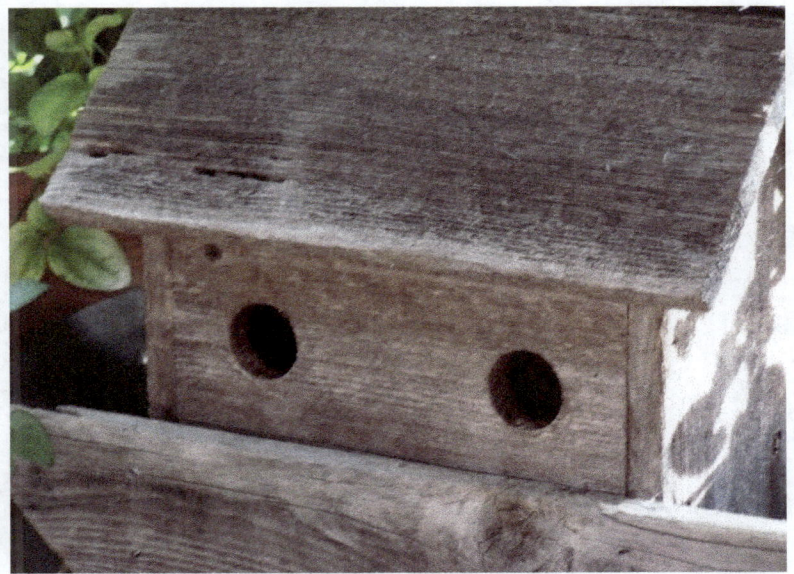

Birds use this as a house made by man. They may not *need* this house, but it certainly provides a safer place in which little ones are hatched and raised before they fly away.

I believe God is glorified by man building this house. He wants us to care about the birds of the air as He does. "'Look at the birds of the air: they neither sow nor reap nor gather into barns, and yet your heavenly Father feeds them'" (Matthew 6:26a). Part of the protection of the birds includes having a safe place for them to feed their babies.

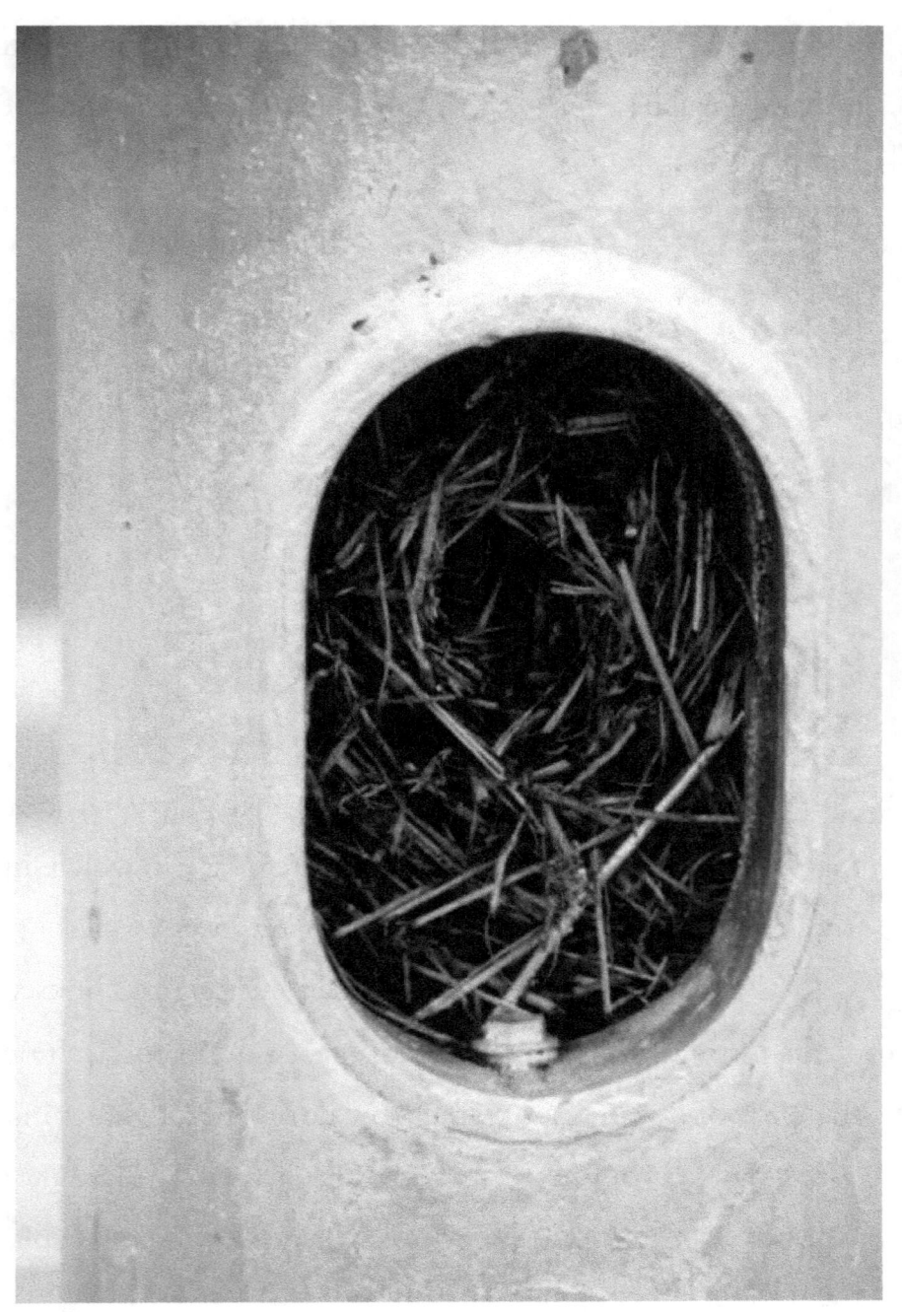

"As they were going along the road, someone said to him, 'I will follow you wherever you go.' And Jesus said to him, 'Foxes have holes, and birds of the air have nests, but the Son of Man has nowhere to lay his head'" (Luke 9:57-58).

When Jesus began His ministry, He did not have a house in which to rest. Birds have made unlikely use of man-made items to build nests. As Jesus traveled, He laid His head wherever, ministering to people, bringing His message of Good News. I was struck by the birds' ingenuity of using this hole in a pole to make the nest in which the baby birds could be kept somewhat safe.

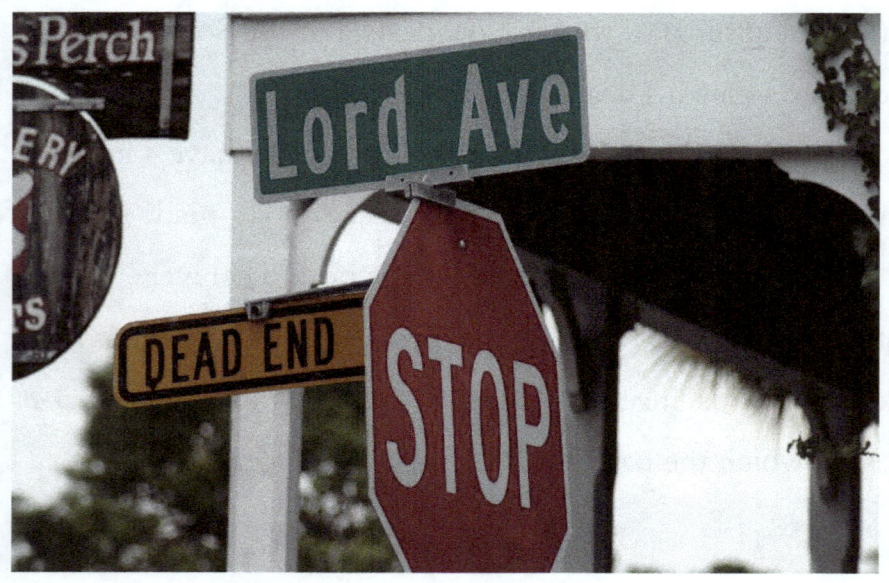

5

One of my favorite signs tells us to stop: it's a dead end unless we rely upon the Lord!

> Only let your manner of life be worthy of the gospel of Christ, so that whether I come and see you or am absent, I may hear of you that you are standing firm in one spirit, with one mind striving side by side for the faith of the gospel, and not frightened in anything by your opponents. This is a clear sign to them of their destruction, but of your salvation, and that from God." (Philippians 1:27-28)

God provides signs to see and follow. I look for signs along the road of life, signs made by man and those provided by God when He tells us of impending danger and/or impending *joy*. Signs are important for us to pay close attention to.

"Behold, the nations are like a drop from a bucket..." (Isaiah 40:15). A foretaste of Jesus' coming is stated in Numbers 24:7 – "'Water shall flow from his buckets, and his seed shall be in many waters; his king shall be higher than Agag, and his kingdom shall be exalted.'"

I believe this points to our Lord and Savior – Jesus Christ. The words speak simply to what Jesus accomplished for us. The Lord's Kingdom should be exalted beyond *all* man-made kingdoms. Living water flows from Jesus' buckets. His Seed is present in these waters. This Truth is life-giving to man.

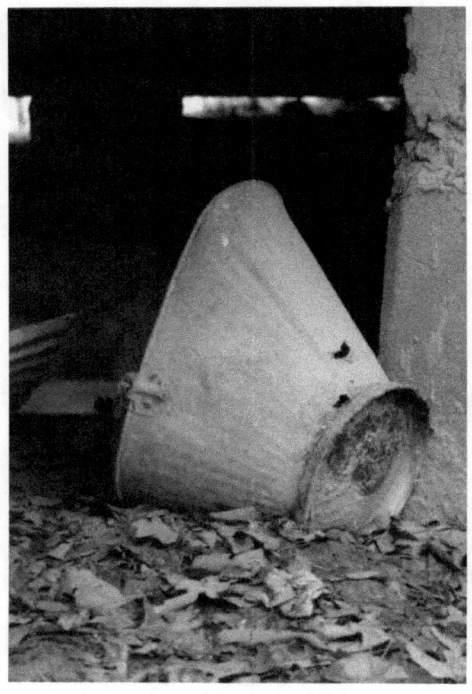

"But we have this treasure in jars of clay, to show that the surpassing power belongs to God and not to us" (2 Corinthians 4:7). This photograph shows a potter's messy hands, creating something from the clay God has provided. We are compared to jars of clay, created by God. His Hands may not be quite so messy as He forms us from His never-ending quantity of clay; however, He does not throw *us* away if we get messy on our life journeys.

I used to believe, if God was not thrilled with our human outcomes or accomplishments, He would indeed throw us in the dump. I no longer believe God sees us this way. I believe He continues to form us, even as we make our mistakes. He is not done until He *says* He is done. We are not thrown out with the bath water, so to speak. God continues to form us as He created us.

We are continually formed and loved into our final forms. We are defined as treasures in clay. God sees our potential far sooner than we can because He knew us before we were even physically born. He does know the plans He has for us. He does not intend to toss out His human creations. He loves His children too much for such a tragic end to our existence.

This is encouraging to me for so many reasons. I have made too many mistakes. *I* would have thrown me out long ago. God is not a human. Thank *Him* for this. His vision extends

far beyond where we may be today. He sees it all. Everything —
the past, the present, and the future. We can rely upon His
omniscience to carry us to eternal life with Him as His beloved
children.

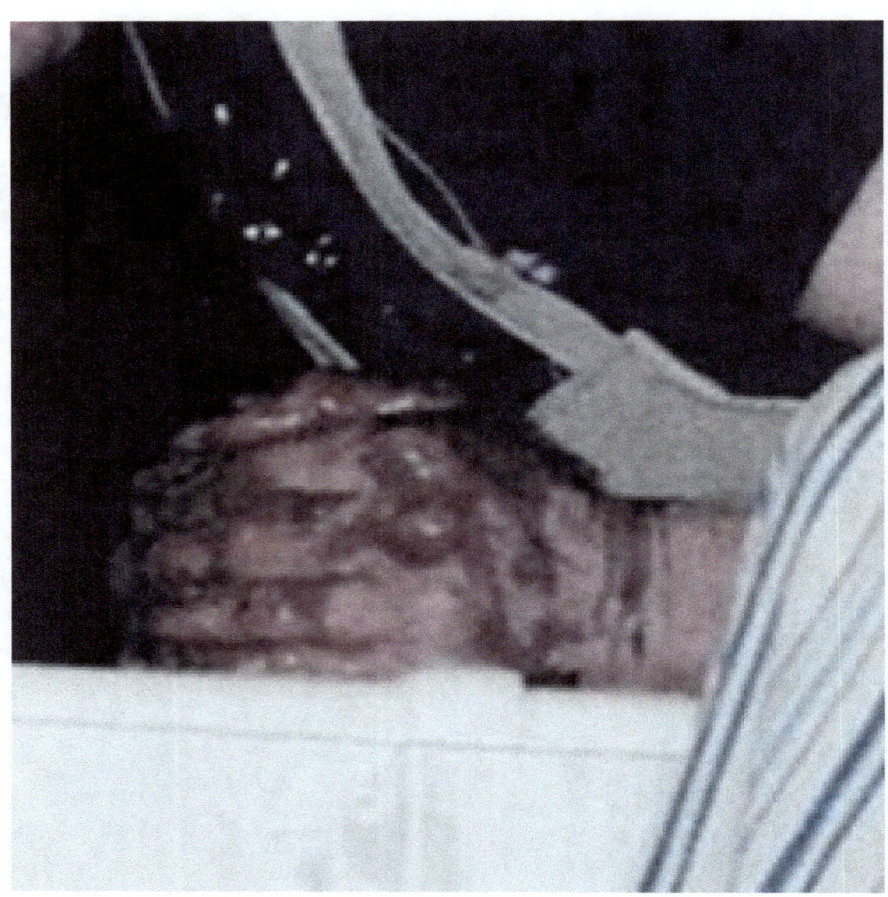

A mast is made by man for use on a ship. It is essential to aid the ship in its travels. God even speaks of the making of a mast: "'"They made all your planks of fir trees from Senir; they took a cedar from Lebanon to make a mast for you"'" (Ezekiel 27:5).

God provided the trees from which masts were formed by man. Again, *everything* was created by God. Man has been given the ability to take God-created substances, form them into useful objects, and make them for the glory of *God*.

A mast is a prime example of man using God-given materials to create something for man's use. I never tire of admiring boats' masts lining a water-front dock. Stately sky-pointers – all saluting the heavens, reminding me to turn my own gaze upward – toward the God Who created the heavens.

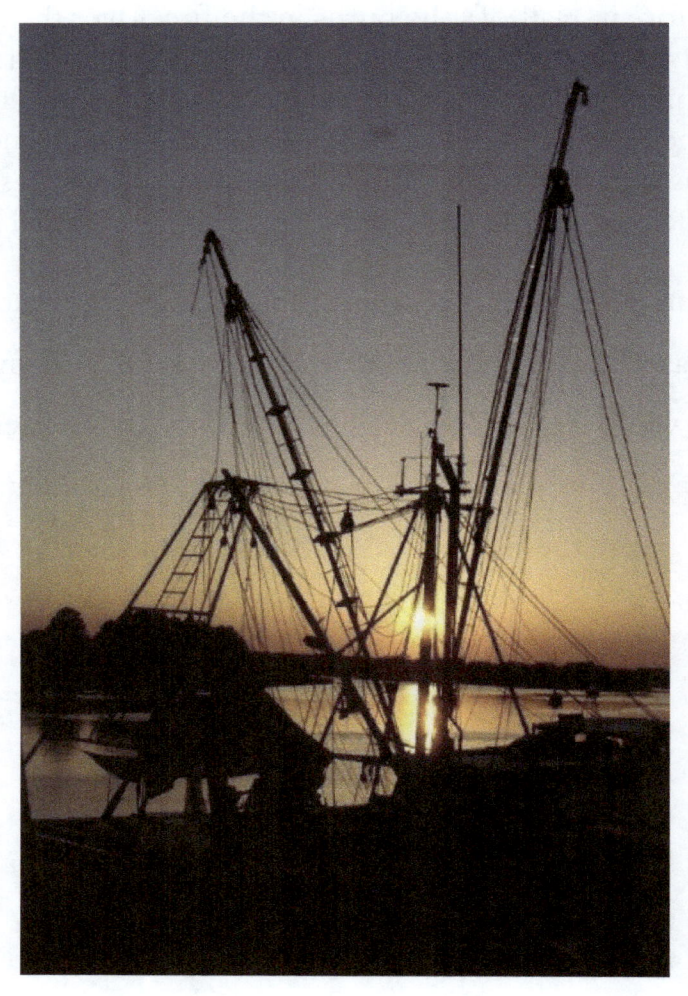

71

He cuts down cedars, or he chooses a cypress tree or an oak and lets it grow strong among the trees of the forest. He plants a cedar and the rain nourishes it. Then it becomes fuel for a man. He takes a part of it and warms himself; he kindles a fire and bakes bread. Also he makes a god and worships it; he makes it an idol and falls down before it. Half of it he burns in the fire. Over the half he eats meat; he roasts it and is satisfied. Also he warms himself and says, "Aha, I am warm, I have seen the fire!" And the rest of it he makes into a god, his idol, and falls down to it and worships it. He prays to it and says, "Deliver me, for you are my god"! (Isaiah 44:14-17)

Man discovered how to find and use fuel for motors. God-created gas provides a way to travel. How far could the motor-less ships sail without gas? They were unable, until much later, to make it to the Americas. God provided the gas and human ingenuity to use the fuel to enable motors to run.

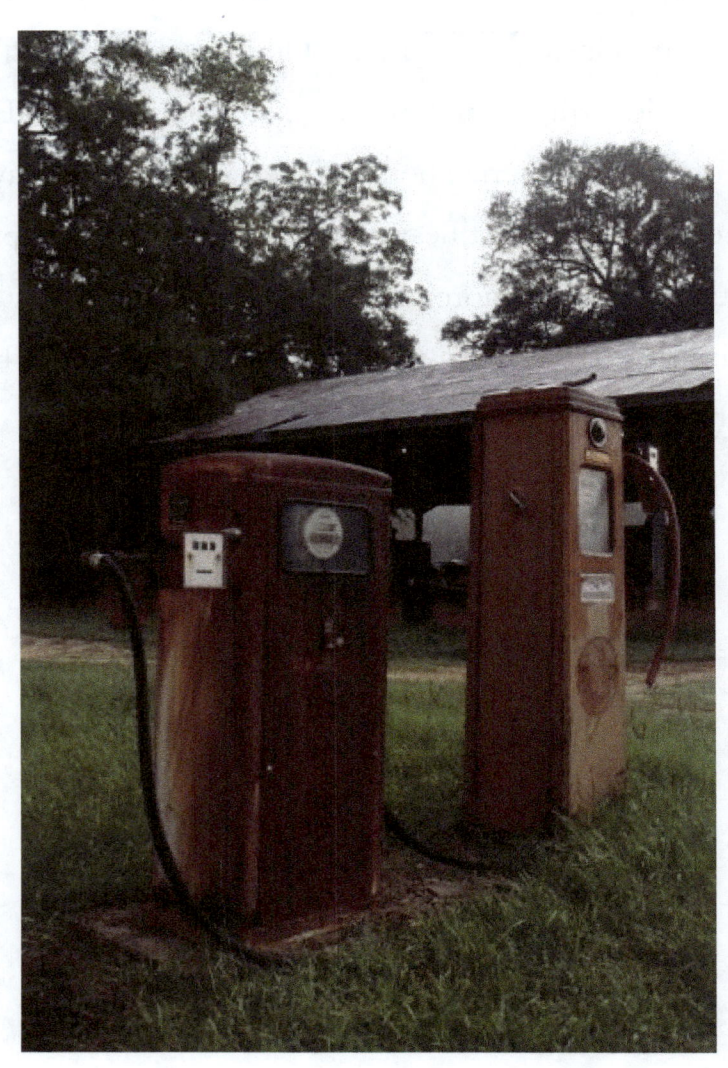

Ministers and missionaries worldwide utilize bicycles, not requiring gas, to carry God's Word. Man was told to care for God's earth, including caring for God-given resources.

This earth, created by God, is for our use until He creates a new earth as our eternal home. "Then I saw a new heaven and a new earth, for the first heaven and the first earth had passed away, and the sea was no more. And I saw the holy city, new Jerusalem, coming down out of heaven from God, prepared as a bride adorned for her husband" (Revelation 21:1-2).

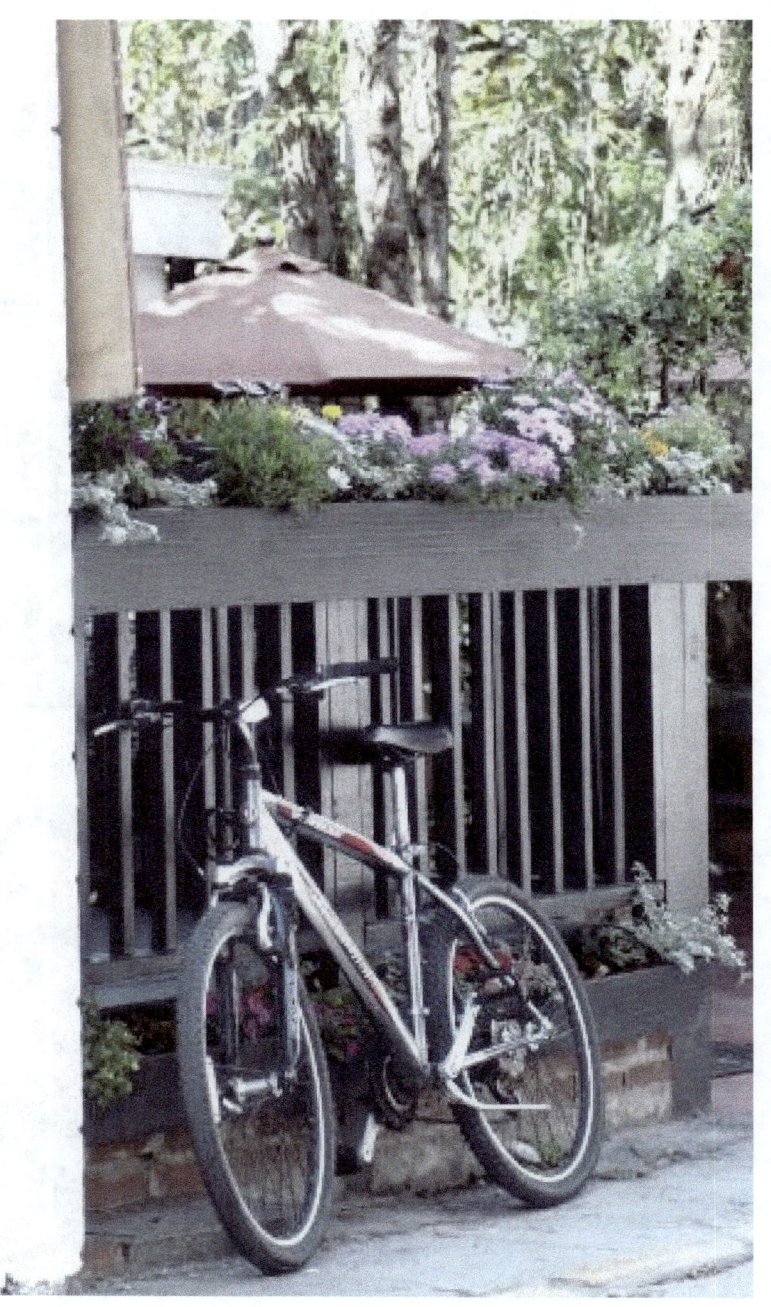

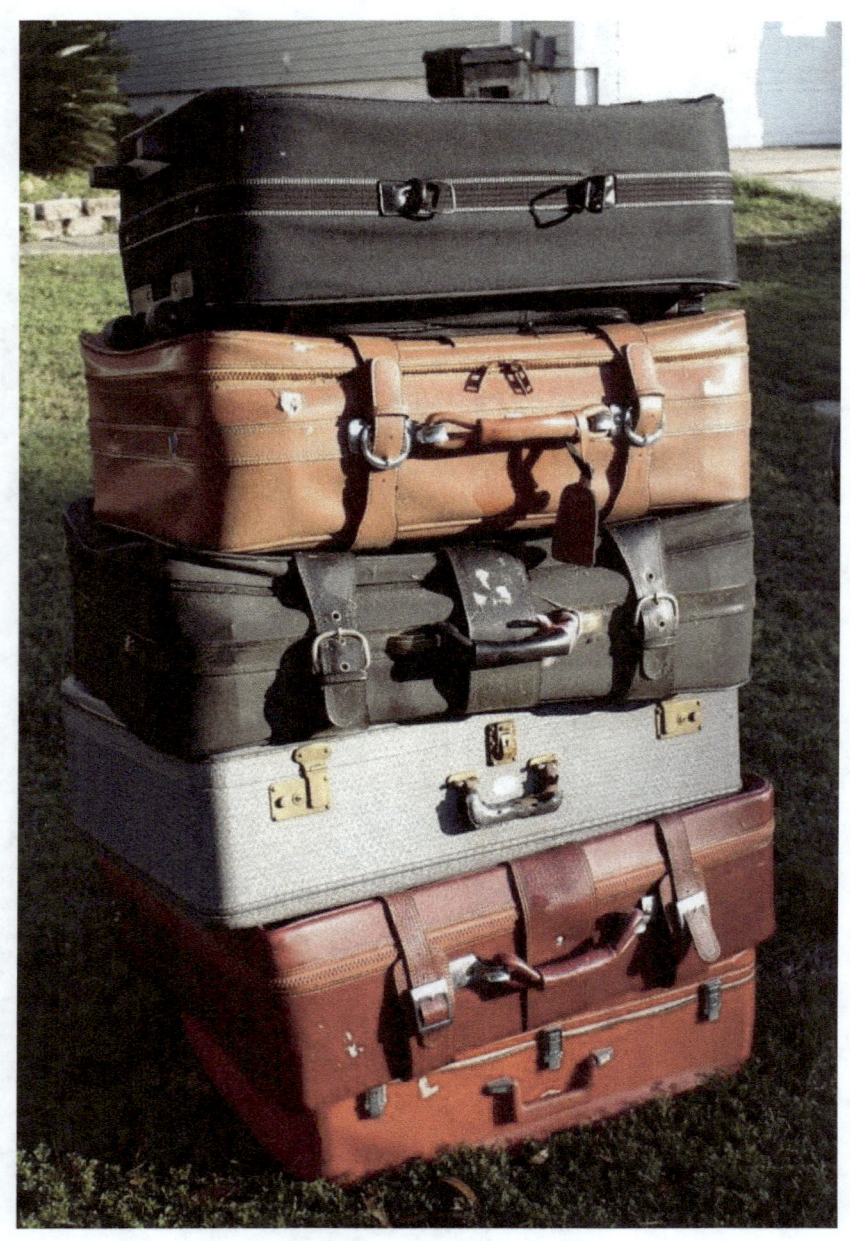

We can carry a lot of baggage, causing us to have too much. What if your sins and transgressions were tied up into a bag never to be seen again? "'For then you would number my steps; you would not keep watch over my sin; my transgression would be sealed up in a bag, and you would cover over my iniquity'" (Job 14:16-17). This is exactly what Jesus did when He took our sins (baggage) upon the Cross.

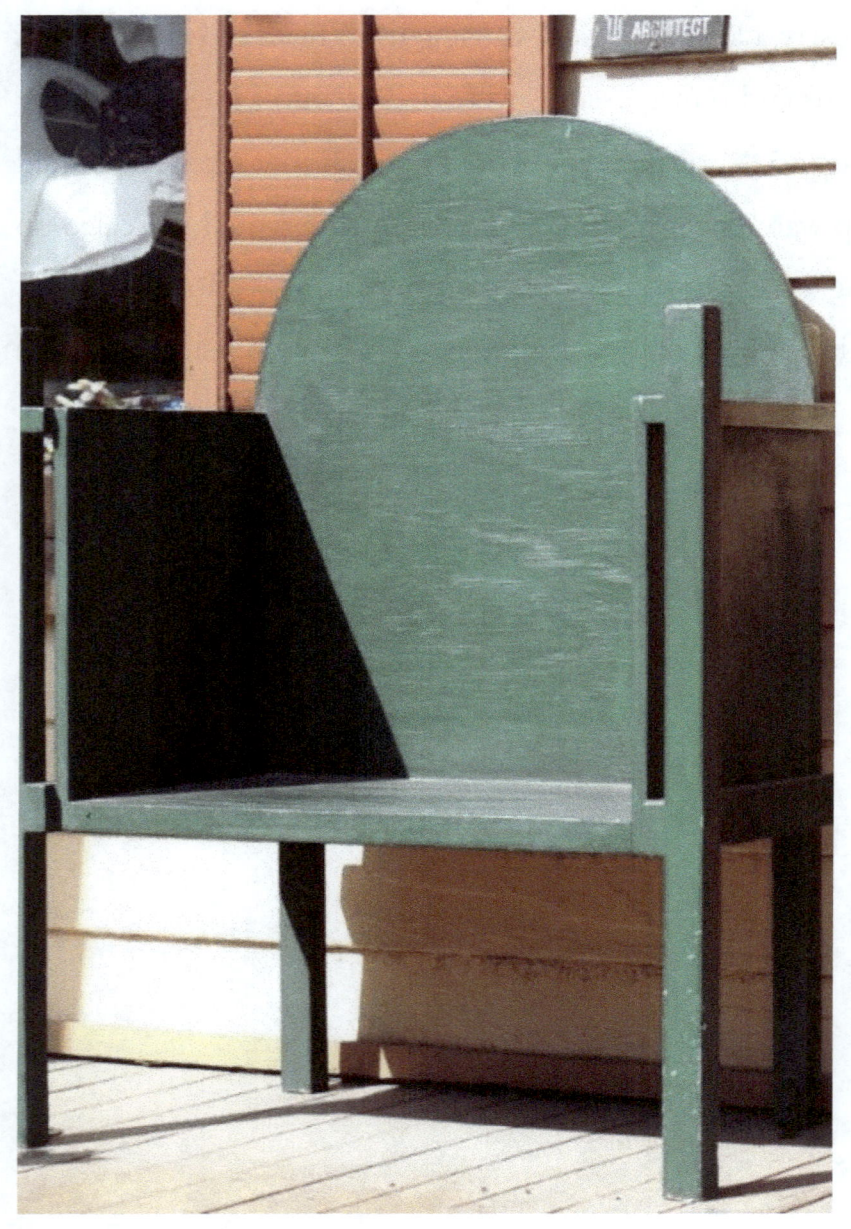

Elisha was a holy man of God (See 2 Kings 4:9). A wealthy woman cared for him. She told her husband, "'Let us make a small room on the roof with walls and put there for him a bed, a table, a chair, and a lamp, so that whenever he comes to us, he can go in there'" (2 Kings 4:10).

Can you imagine how great the Lord's throne is? I was struck by the uncomfortable look of this chair. I believe God's throne is plush and comfortable and utilized well as He watches over us *all* from it.

Jesus' throne at God's right is no less comfortable or used for anything less important than the one the Father sits upon.

"Stand therefore, having fastened on the belt of truth, and having put on the breastplate of righteousness, and as shoes for your feet, having put on the readiness given by the gospel of peace" (Ephesians 6:14-15). Travel was important to those carrying the Gospel to the world. Strong shoes were needed to keep feet from being injured or worn down. This photograph seems to be telling us shoes don't last forever; however, God's love and His Word and message do. Our need to keep shoes on our feet to carry His gospel of peace to a weary world is also to be done so long as we are on this earth. Yet I often need newer shoes to carry my feet forward to declare the Good News of the Gospel of Jesus Christ.

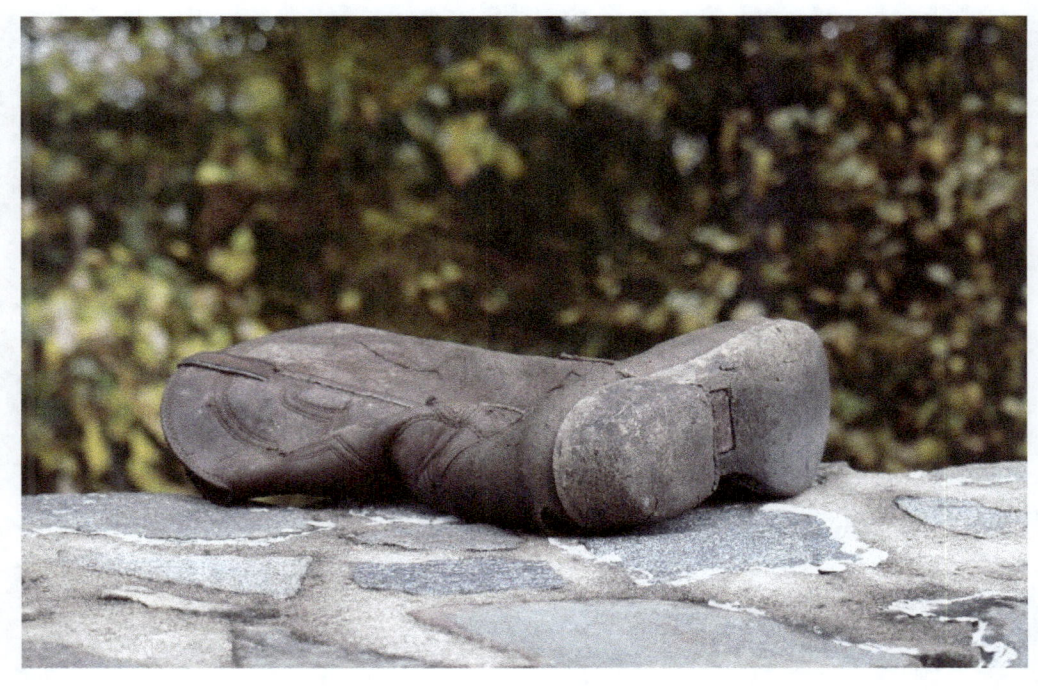

"'I baptize you with water for repentance, but he who is coming after me is mightier than I, whose sandals I am not worthy to carry. He will baptize you with the Holy Spirit and fire'" (Matthew 3:11). John the Baptist knew Jesus was God's Son, worthy to be glorified on earth even as He is in heaven.

Sandals were worn by first century people. They were essential to those who wore them daily. When people wore sandals, their feet became dirty.

Jesus washed His Disciples' feet on the night before His crucifixion. Peter was appalled that He would do this. But He knew how important it was for their feet to be washed. He also knew how important it was for their sins to be cleansed by Him, through His death and resurrection. He physically washed their feet, then cleansed their souls with His life, death, and resurrection.

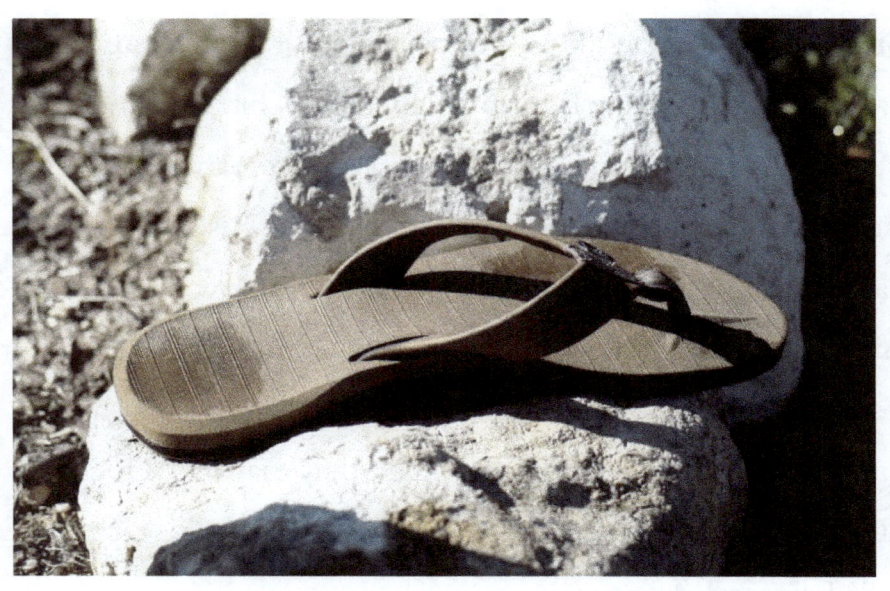

"'Whoever causes one of these little ones who believes in me to sin, it would be better for him if a great millstone were hung around his neck and he were thrown into the sea'" (Mark 9:42). This seems like a harsh Word from Jesus. But it is so important for children to be cared for, not neglected or mistreated. Too many people neglect and mistreat children. Christians must be prepared to care for these little ones. I am so sorry if you have had a hard life. God knows this. He cares for His children, no matter the age. "You shall not mistreat any widow or fatherless child. If you do mistreat them, and they cry out to me, I will surely hear their cry" (Exodus 22:22-23). Children don't often have a voice, to express the fear under which they may live. Does this millstone image impact us when warning people to treat children well? I sincerely hope so.

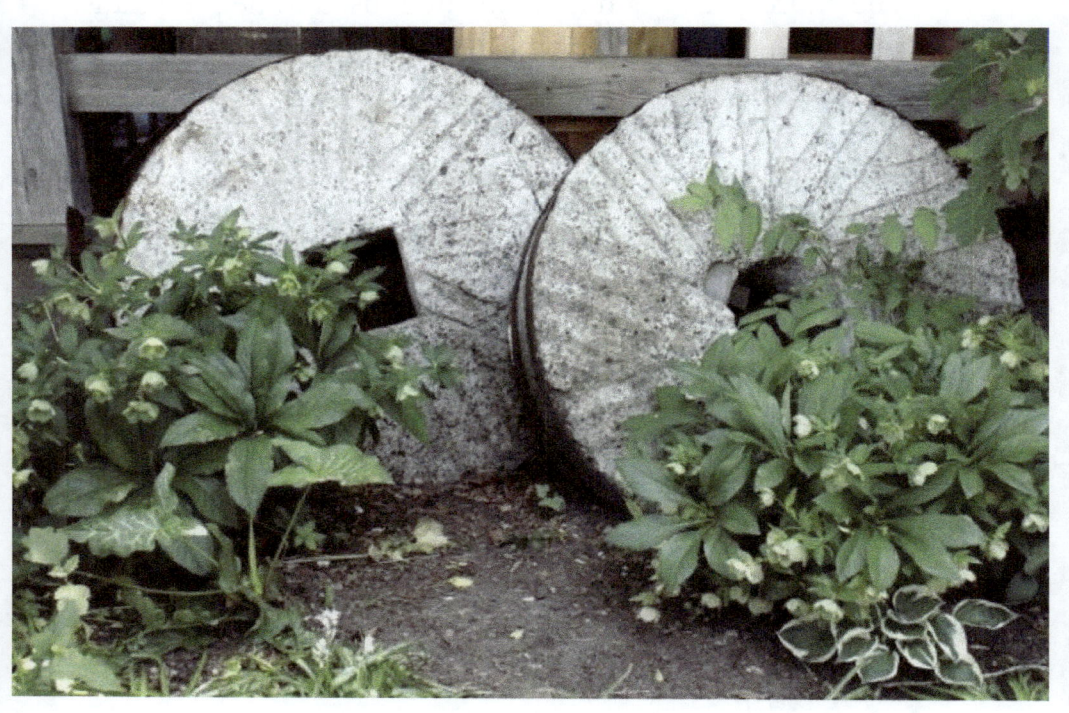

"He will raise a signal for nations far away, and whistle for them from the ends of the earth; and behold, quickly, speedily they come!" (Isaiah 5:26). A church bell serves as a signal for several reasons. It keeps time for people. It can signal of a town emergency.

The church bell is a man-made item used to help humans. God created the material by which it is formed and created. Yet it is far more than simply a pile of metal with a ringer hanging from its middle.

How does God signal His people? Isaiah tells us He may even whistle for His children. I always thought it a bit odd for God to whistle for His people; however, He gave us the ability to whistle so He has even created the whistle to be used as a signal when needed.

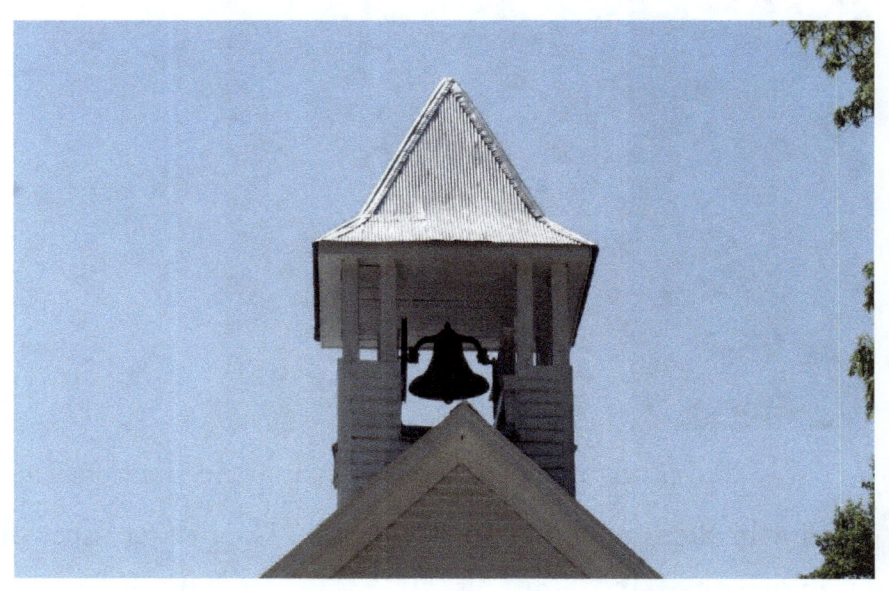

A man-made whistle may be used to alert others of danger. I carry this whistle with me when I go out alone. Being a woman can be a scary event, if traveling alone and with little to no protection. God protects us, though. He is our Savior, our Redeemer, our Lord.

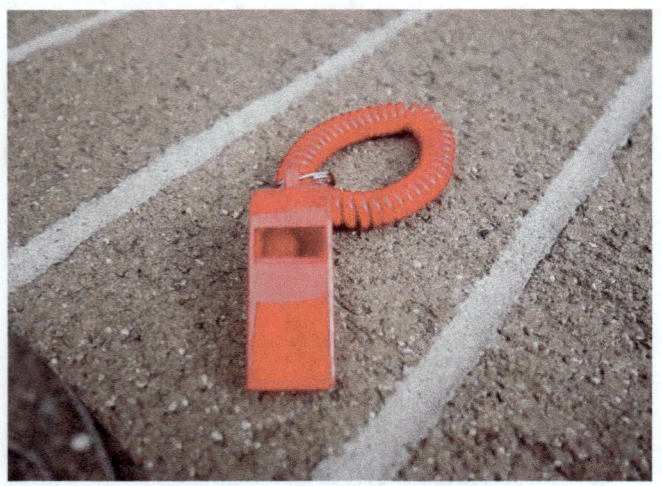

When humans travel alone, they may need a physical, man-made whistle to blow in an emergency. "The prudent sees danger and hides himself, but the simple go on and suffer for it" (Proverbs 22:3, 27:12).

When we are alerted to danger, what do we do? Do we go on ahead and potentially suffer or are we prudent and hide ourselves appropriately? Prudence is a God-given character to which we should listen and appropriately react.

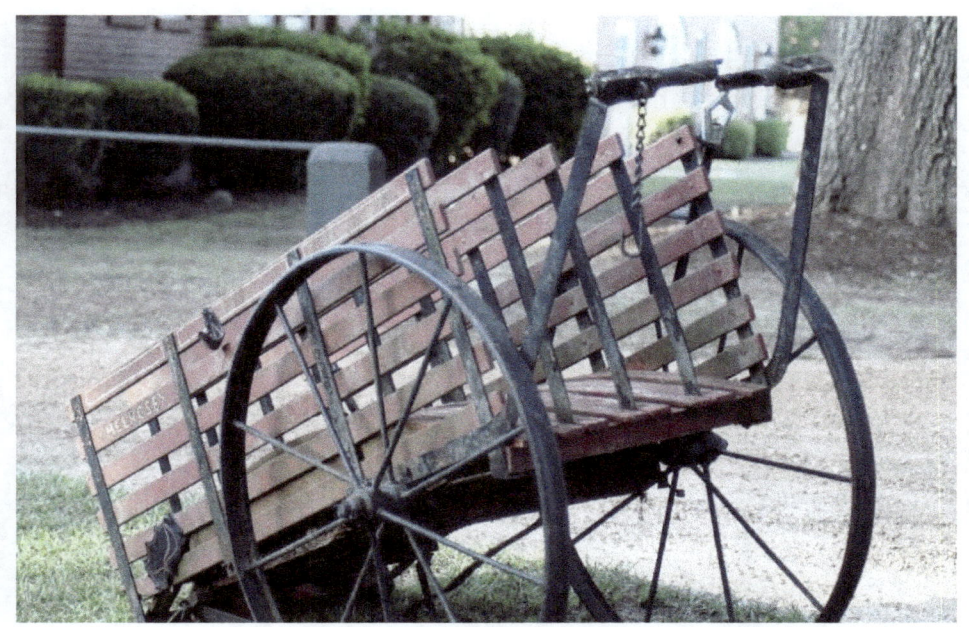

Was the ark of the covenant carried in a vehicle resembling this? Probably not exactly like this but maybe close. The ark is not lost to us. "Then God's temple in heaven was opened, and the ark of his covenant was seen within his temple. There were flashes of lightning, rumblings, peals of thunder, an earthquake, and heavy hail" (Revelation 11:19). This verse clearly tells us the ark is residing safely inside God's holy temple. This fact brings us comfort, if we believe in the God of the universe Who keeps all His treasures, including us, safe. We are treasured by Him, protected, and given all we need for our lives on earth. and so is His ark of the covenant.

The implication of His protection is *awesome*.

"And he dreamed, and behold, there was a ladder set up on the earth, and the top of it reached to heaven. And behold, the angels of God were ascending and descending on it" (Genesis 28:12). Angels used a ladder to ascend and descend from heaven to earth.

We use ladders to gain access to places higher than we may reach. I doubt God would have allowed man to invent them if we had no need for them. He knew we would build structures and climb trees which were higher than our reach. What an ingenious item is a ladder when we need extra height to ascend and descend, just as the angels did from heaven to earth.

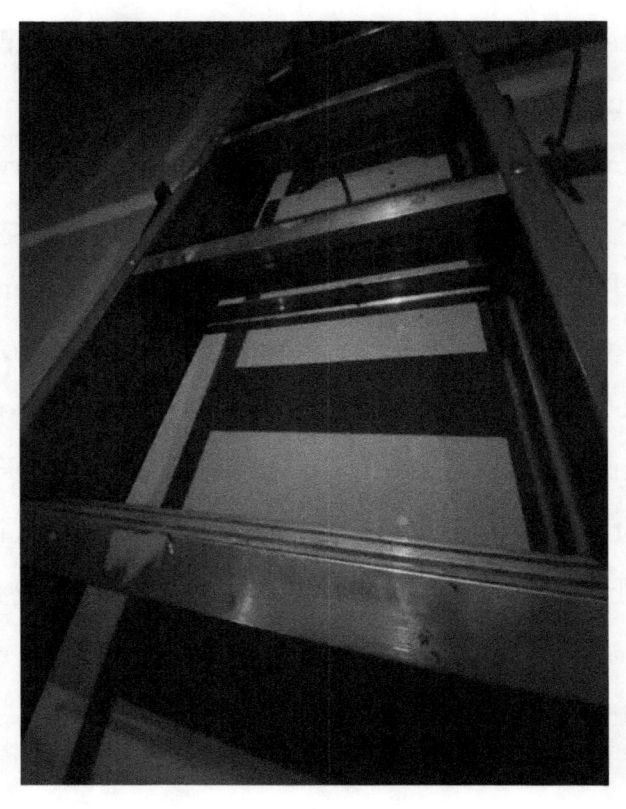

When Jesus walked on earth, cars were not invented. Today, our major form of travel is by car. We revere our cars almost excessively.

Paul traveled extensively on earth, without use of a car. Commending Titus, he said, "And not only that, but he has been appointed by the churches to travel with us as we carry out this act of grace that is being ministered by us, for the glory of the Lord himself and to show our good will" (2 Corinthians 8:19).

Today, ministry travel by foot or car is meant to carry out God's grace for His glory, just as Paul did mostly by foot and ship. Is your car a status symbol or a means of getting from one spot to another? We admire when someone drives up in a brand-new car. What would Jesus drive if He were on earth? He probably would make use of His feet to travel. That's what God created them for. Right?

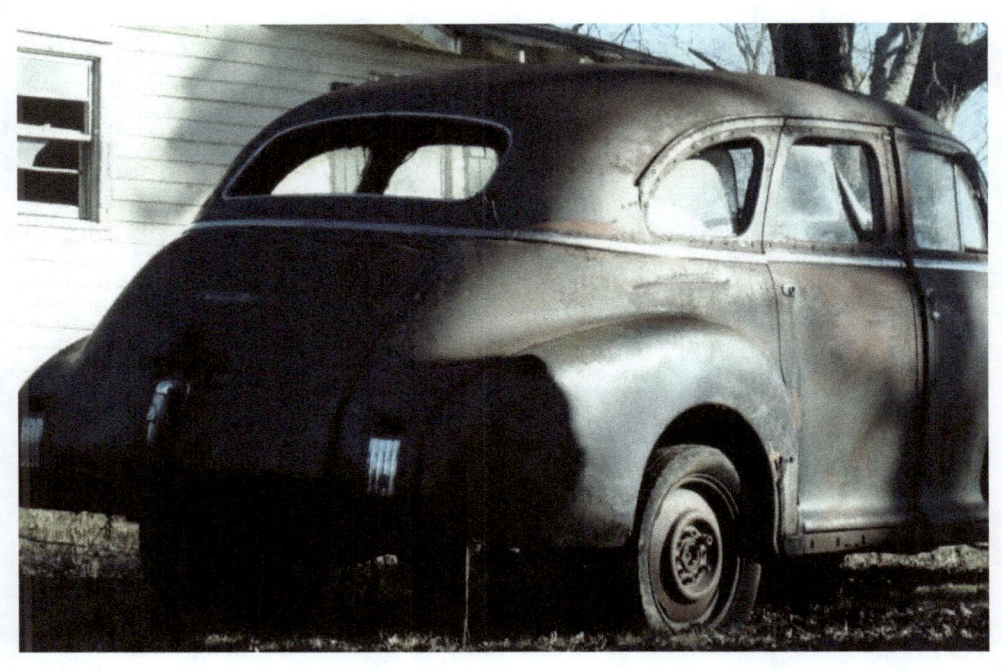

We make use of several means of travel as we minister to individuals around the world. "She makes linen garments and sells them; she delivers sashes to the merchant" (Proverbs 31:24). All for the *glory* of God.

Today trains are likely the way many linen garments and people are shipped. Have you ever sat at a railroad crossing, watching too many to count cars rolling by you? Do you wonder what they carry? I do. Trains are indispensable to many people, hoping to ship their goods to places around the country.

Merchants rely upon trains to deliver the items they hope to sell. People have used God-given material to make these wonderful traveling trains. Travelers can carry God's greater message via trains.

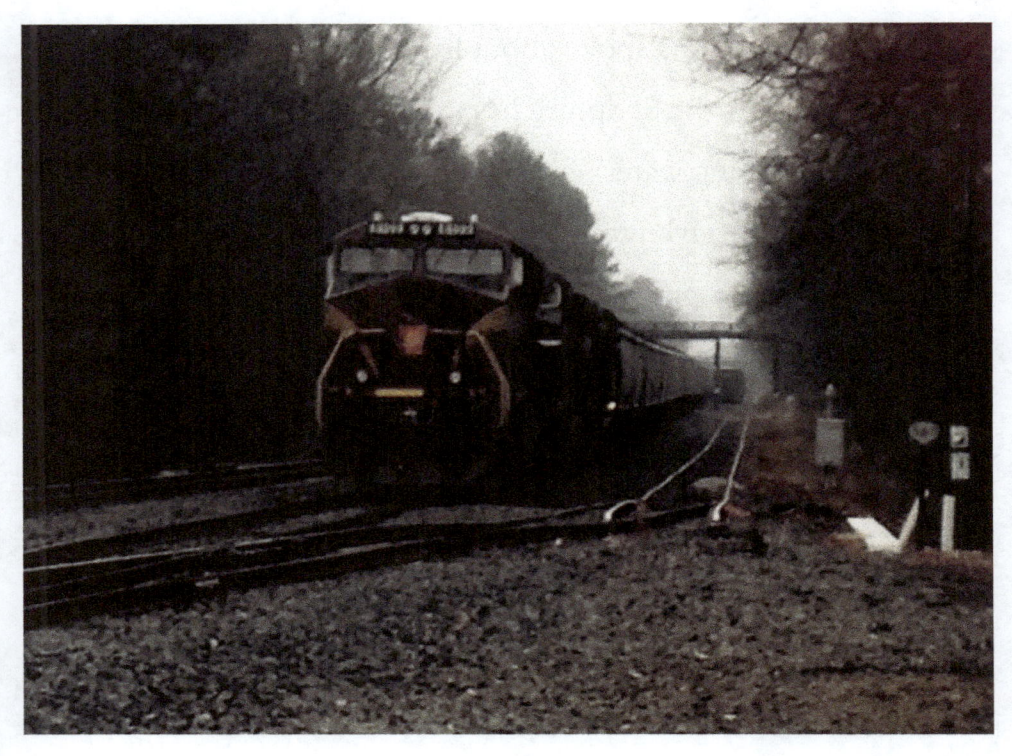

Without water man would simply not survive. We make our own types of monuments to water, including beautiful water fountains. Jeremiah speaks of "the Lord, the fountain of living water" (See Jeremiah 17:13). Jesus spoke about living water, "'Whoever believes in me, as the Scripture has said, "Out of his heart will flow rivers of living water"'" (John 7:38). He was speaking of the Holy Spirit, to be given to man from God.

What better gift could God give to man than life-giving water for our bodies and for our souls?

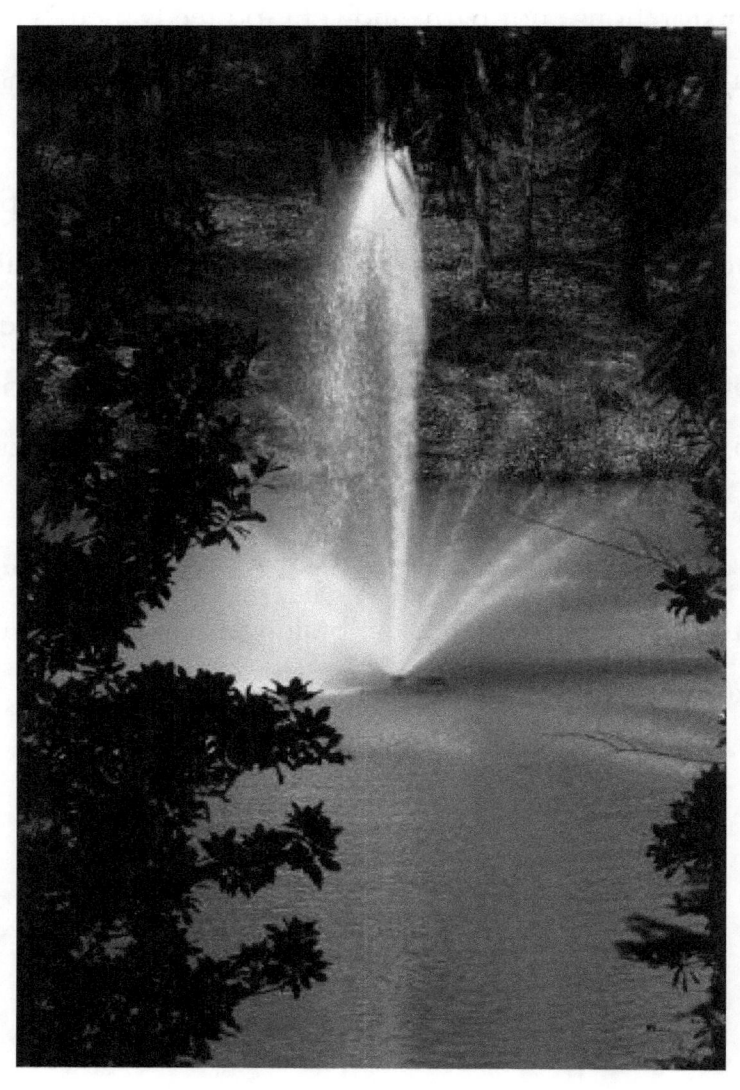

"'Consider the ravens: they neither sow nor reap, they have neither storehouse nor barn, and yet God feeds them'" (Luke 12:24a). Barns are used by man to store grain, feed, animals, machinery, and anything else needing a dry place.

Birds and animals do not build barns. They rely upon man and God to provide a barn to receive shelter, when possible. God created the trees from which the wood is derived to build barns. Do you think about how crucial a barn is to man and those for whom it is provided? Do you watch birds flying in and out of barns, building nests and bringing food to their babies?

Sometimes a bird may simply use a barn for its own shelter from rain or snow or wind. Man builds barns used by man and beast alike.

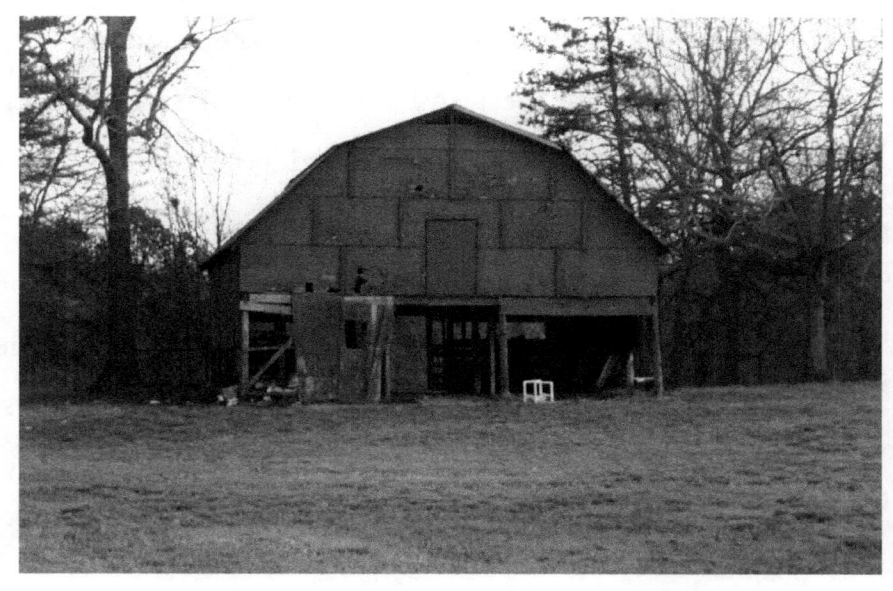

"You crown the year with your bounty; your wagon tracks overflow with abundance" (Psalm 65:11). Man-made railroad tracks were used to carry items via trains. Often train tracks were built atop wagon tracks as he traveled into the wilderness.

What would the western United States have been like without the use of trains to bring needed items to them as they settled into their towns and their churches?

God provided the steel. Men shaped them into the form they needed to make straight train tracks, but God is the One Who created the steel. What a miracle of our God to create steel we have found useful in the making of train tracks and many other items.

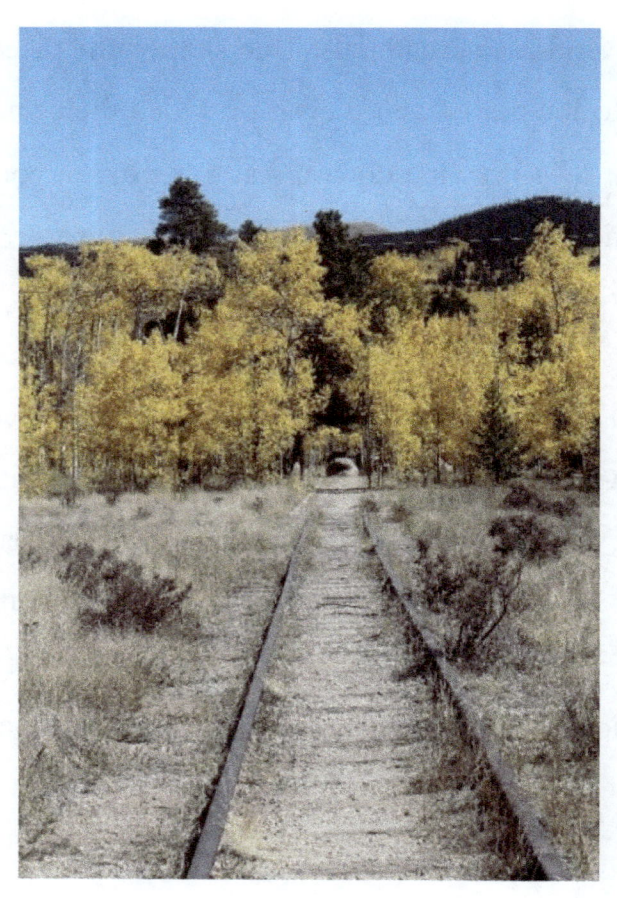

6

Men created games to amuse themselves, learn strategies, and increase their abilities to think. The boards and game pieces are made from God-made materials. Men shaped the pieces to mean something to the players. God even provided their imagination to create them. "'"[O]n what do you rest this trust of yours? Do you think that mere words are strategy and power for war? In whom do you now trust, that you have rebelled against me?"'" (2 Kings 18:19c-20).

We use our God-given ability to strategize so we can play the games. Games may be competitive or fun. No matter how we approach it, we do need to strategize about how to play.

How well do we use our brains to strategize our next move in our lives? Do we turn to the Lord for the next best thing we can do to glorify Him? Seems like a good strategy, doesn't it?

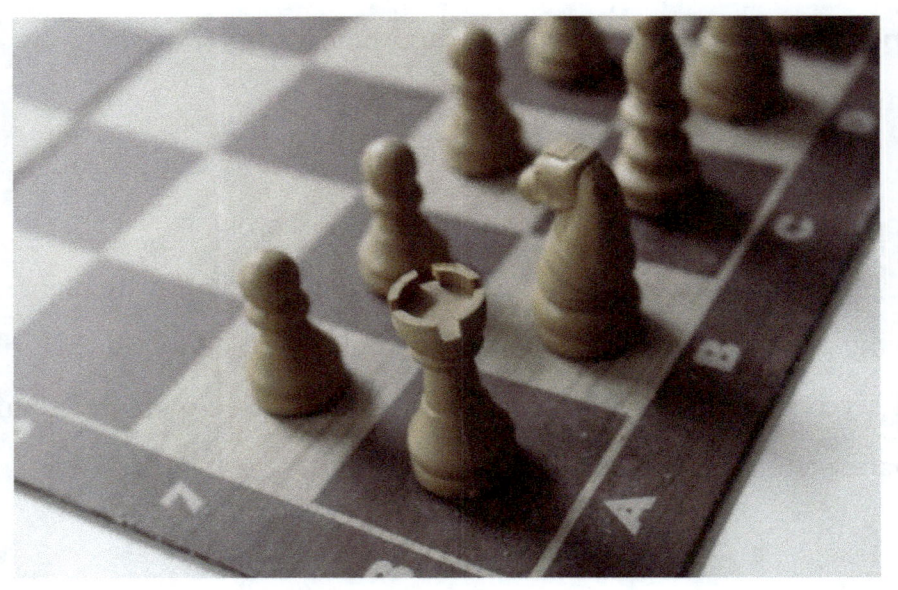

Jesus spoke to the Pharisees and said, "'Truly, truly, I say to you, he who does not enter the sheepfold by the door but climbs in by another way, that man is a thief and a robber. But he who enters by the door is the shepherd of the sheep. To him the gatekeeper opens. The sheep hear his voice, and he calls his own sheep by name and leads them out'" (John 10:1-3).

Doors keep us out and keep us in. What we see through a door's windows reveal sights otherwise unseen.

Do you think God sees our ability to miraculously plant living things for our use? God is certainly glorified by our planting of seeds to create living items for food and for enjoyment in our man-made greenhouses.

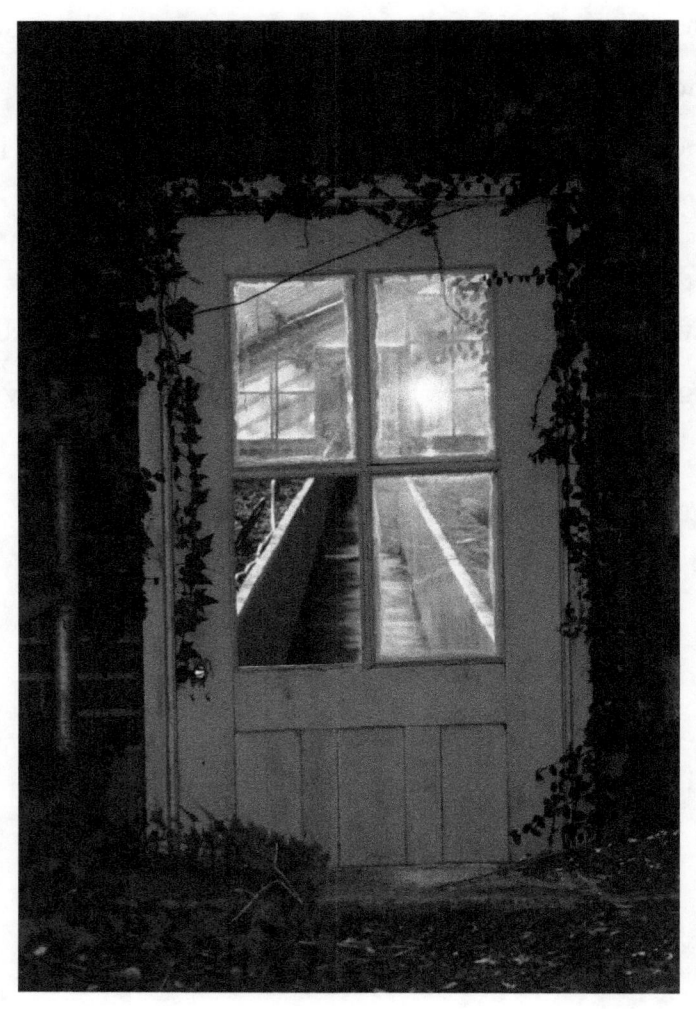

Rivers were difficult to cross especially after the advent of horses and buggies and cars driven by people needing travel to cross. Man made covered bridges to provide the way. Some of these bridges remain for us to admire and use. The covered bridges I can still see remind me of the ingenious ways man has used his talents and abilities to solve problems.

There is another shelter, though. "He who dwells in the shelter of the Most High will abide in the shadow of the Almighty. I will say to the LORD, 'My refuge and my fortress, my God, in whom I trust'" (Psalm 91:1-2). The Lord is our shelter, protecting us from harm. What a *fantastic* shelter He provides for our souls.

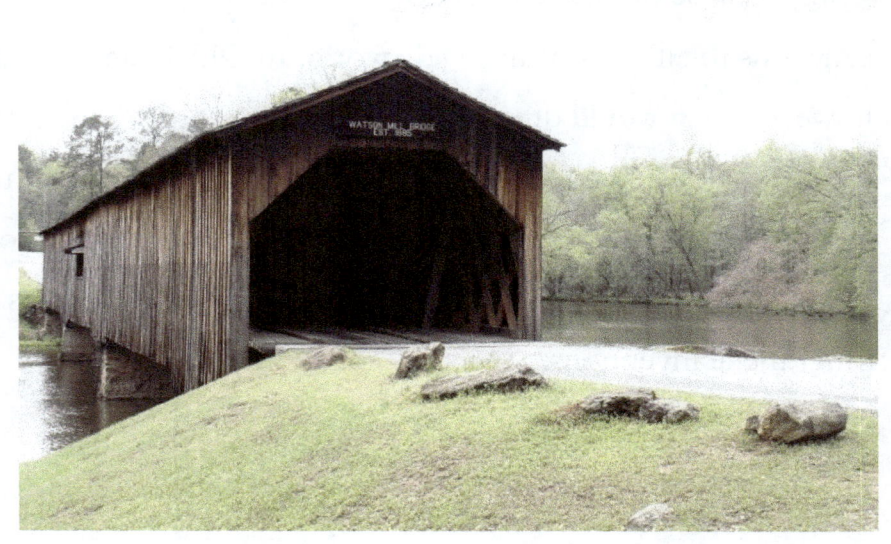

The hot air balloon. What a way to observe God's *beautiful* world. I envy those who crawl into the basket, flying away to see the world spread out below them as they soar in the man-made beauty that is the hot air balloon! "And I say, 'Oh, that I had wings like a dove! I would fly away and be at rest'" (Psalm 55:6).

Why do you think man wants to fly? He saw the birds flying because of how God had created them to travel. Airplanes can jet us to all parts of this wide world. In Old Testament times; however, men would dream of flying like the birds they saw from the ground, making it seem so easy to go from point to point.

The hot air balloon is a beautiful invention for man to experience a small part of flying without the use of airplanes or other metal inventions.

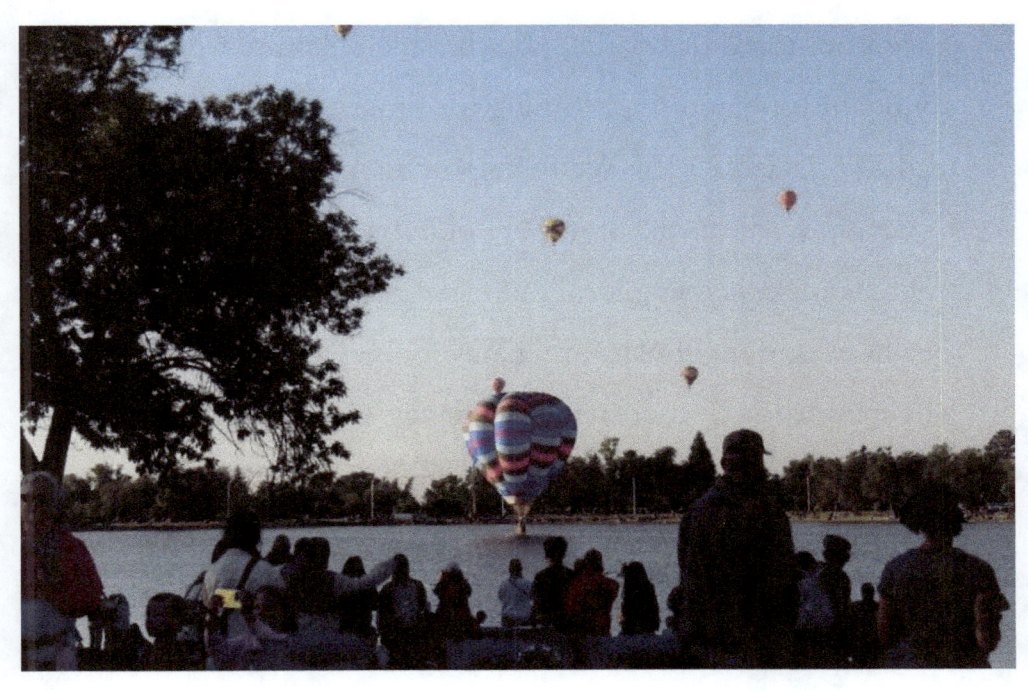

"Her merchandise and her wages will be holy to the Lord. It will not be stored or hoarded, but her merchandise will supply abundant food and fine clothing for those who dwell before the LORD" (Isaiah 23:18). We rely upon man-made merchandise to supply our needs. Stores are built by man to house this merchandise, keeping it safe until we need it for our stomachs, our houses, our animals, or whatever else. Merchandise is made by man from God-created substances. Can you think of how much merchandise may be kept safe in a store? Man made the stores themselves, as storehouses for the merchandise. As we "dwell before the LORD", we are made aware of how diligently God protects the items we may need in our everyday lives.

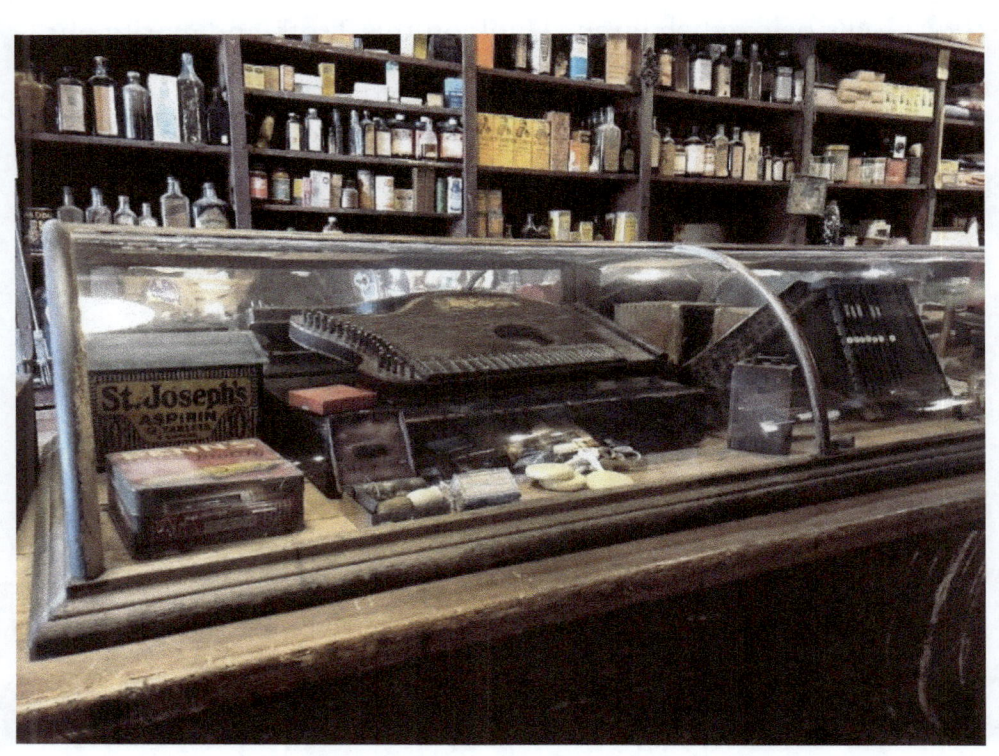

Man-made structures don't last forever. Many items created by man are falling apart, no longer used but not necessarily gone.

God's Creation is here to last for man, though. He will create a new earth upon His return. We will live in His Creation for eternity.

Think about it! Eternity. Forever. Never-ending. For us. For God's beloved children. Think on this Truth and glorify our God with all your praise and song directed to Him.

The most beautiful and elaborate home on earth can *never* compare with the mansions made in Heaven by God for us. John 14:1-4 says:

> Let not your hearts be troubled. Believe in God; believe also in me. In my Father's house are many rooms. If it were not so would I have told you that I go to prepare a place for you? And if I go and prepare a place for you, I will come again and will take you to myself, that where I am you may be also. And you know the way to where I am going.

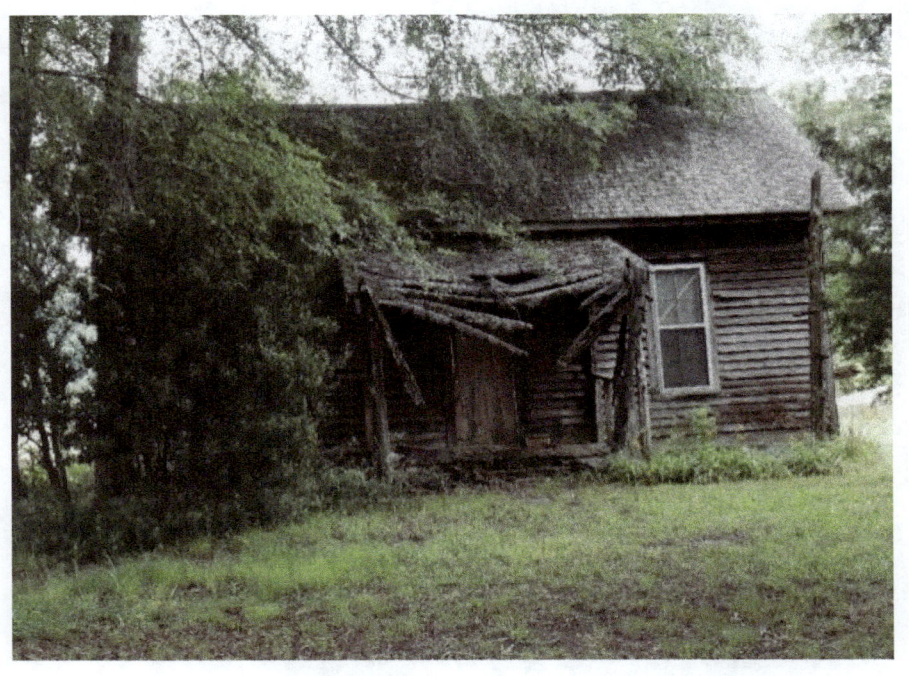

Men have shaped their image of angels using God-created material:

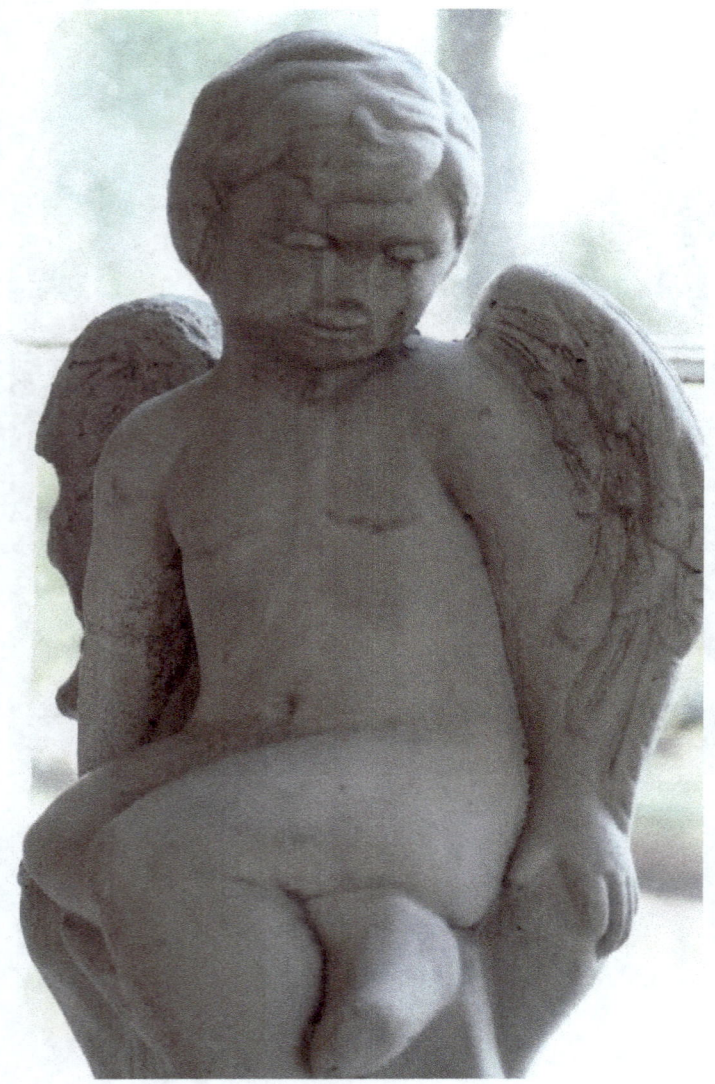

Do you believe this is how angels truly appear? I am not sure myself, but it is the way man has imagined angels. This is a man-made idea of how God's angels appear to the human eye.

Angels play a big part in God's story. They did appear to various people in ancient times. They foretold things. They admonished people sometimes, telling them what God knew to be true. An angel appeared to Mary, telling her about the impending birth of Jesus. Joseph was comforted by an angel as he discovered the truth about Mary's pregnancy. "But as he considered these things, behold, an angel of the Lord appeared to him in a dream, saying 'Joseph, son of David, do not fear to take Mary as your wife, for that which is conceived in her is from the Holy Spirit. She will bear a son, and you shall call his name Jesus, for he will save his people from their sins'" (Matthew 1:20-21).

What would you do if an angel appeared to you? We are told in the Bible individuals who saw angels were immediately told not to be afraid. It would be hard to not be afraid of an angel of the Lord appearing to us, wouldn't it? I don't think this particular angel seems very frightening. Created from some type of stone, it still doesn't cause fear.

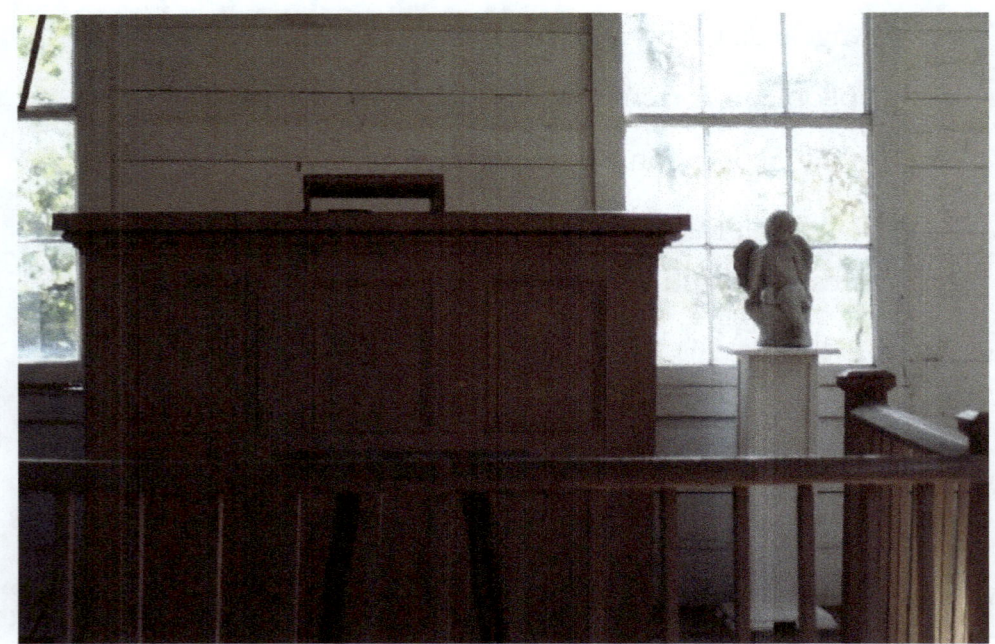

Pulpits are made of God-created wood, shaped to form a raised platform for the preacher to use as his holding place for the Bible and sermon notes. Jesus utilized no pulpit when He preached. His voice carried to all gathered. Today's preacher is ordained to preach the Good News of the Gospel. "'[b]ut the word of the Lord remains forever.' And this word is the good news that was preached to you" (1 Peter 1:25). Pulpits can be made from several materials; however, most are made from wood. God provided the trees for these pulpits to be formed and used by man to preach His Word in such an *elegant* way. Pulpits can also be used to hold the Bible as the preacher speaks the Word to us. This is a grand way to use a God-given material for our use, to glorify Him.

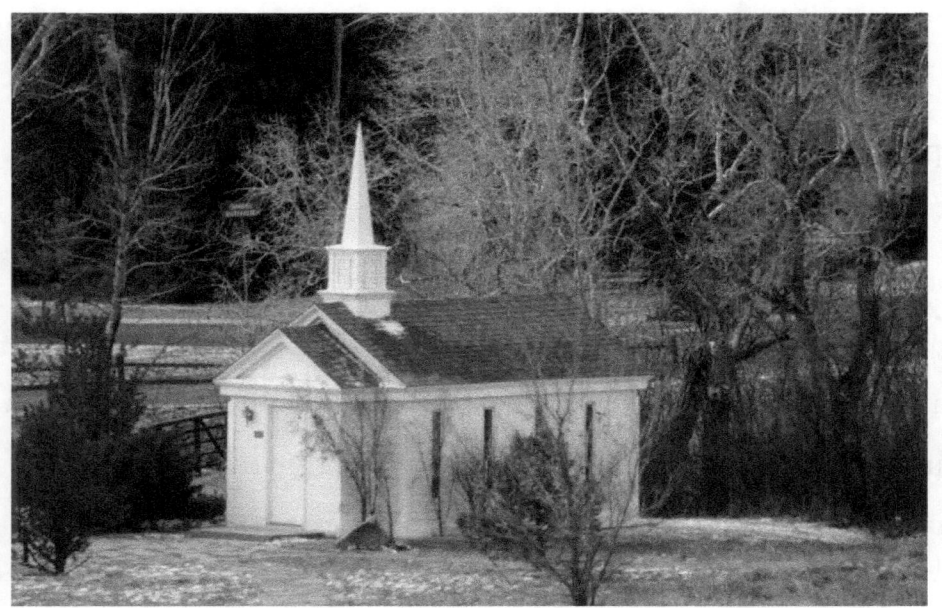

We build churches, large and small, to worship God. They can protect us from weather and serve as seating places for the faithful. The church is far more than a man-made building, though. "[t]he household of God, which is the church of the living God, a pillar and fortress of the truth" (1 Timothy 3:15b-c). Churches are places where we can proclaim our love for the Lord, sing His praises, and testify to His faithfulness. Churches are to be fortresses of God's Truth. Wherever you worship God, remember He created all the material used to build your church.

Churches are often built to impress others. Large, imposing churches may seem more like testaments to man than to God. I believe He is much more glorified by the hearts and service of the people inside the church.

7

"The wind blows to the south and goes around to the north; around and around goes the wind, and on its circuits the wind returns" (Ecclesiastes 1:6). Maybe man thought about the wind going round and round as it blew from every direction. Wheels have been used for centuries to carry items and people inside carts, etc. God created the wind and the mind of man to use materials given by God and to be utilized to serve man.

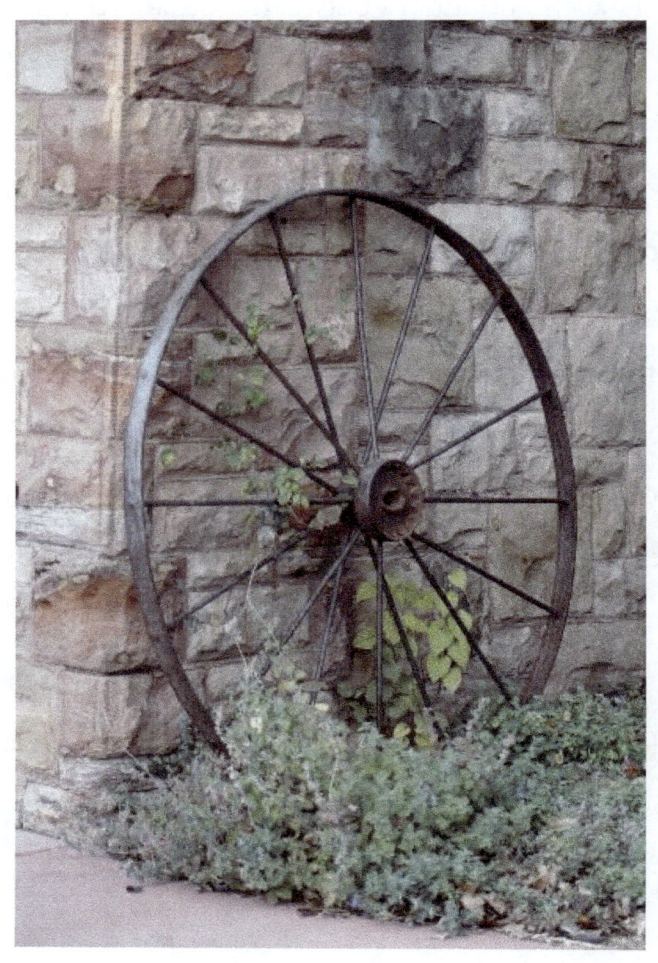

"'He stretches out the north over the void and hangs the earth on nothing. He binds up the waters in his thick clouds, and the cloud is not split open under them. He covers the face of the full moon and spreads over it his cloud. He has inscribed a circle on the face of the waters at the boundary between light and darkness'" (Job 26:7-10).

Circles are used by man in our paintings, on our cars, as prototypes for our wheels, our jar lids, as so many items we use today. Our earth is round, giving us a perfect example of the circle. The sun is round. The moon is round. The circle is extremely important to us as the example for our inventions.

Circles are too numerous to speak about or list. We are surrounded by circles. Basketball and baseball and soccer exist because of the round ball used to play highly competitive sports.

But this does not diminish the importance of the circle in our world. God used a circle shape to make boundaries for water and seas. Think about the many, many uses of the circle and ponder how God created it to be so important.

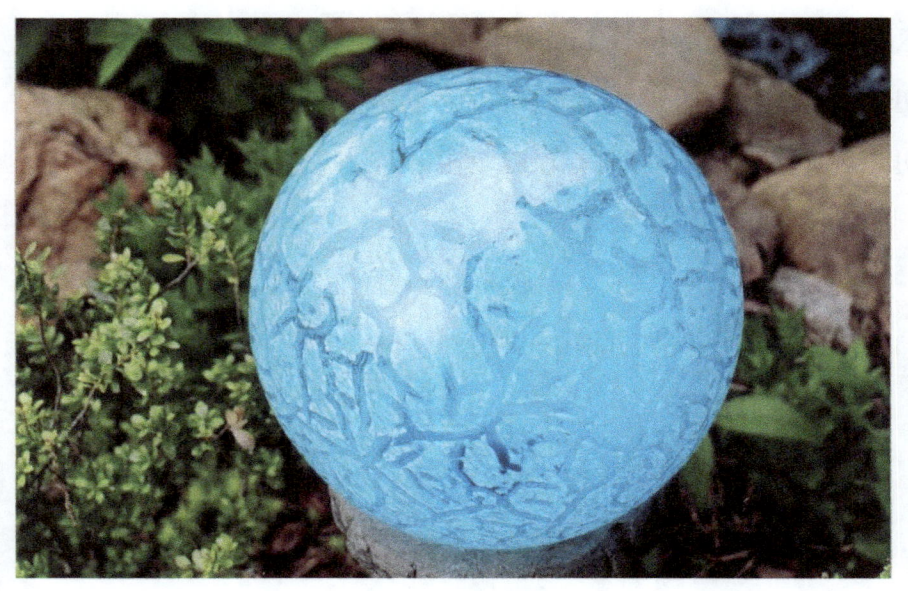

Ah, the bride. The Bible speaks of the bride in such eloquent ways: "'Hallelujah! For the Lord our God the Almighty reigns. Let us rejoice and exult and give him the glory, for the marriage of the Lamb has come, and his Bride has made herself ready; it was granted her to clothe herself with fine linen, bright and pure'" (Revelation 19:6c-8b). The Bride is the church. Human brides who adorn themselves are following in the steps of the church who will adorn itself as God's Bride.

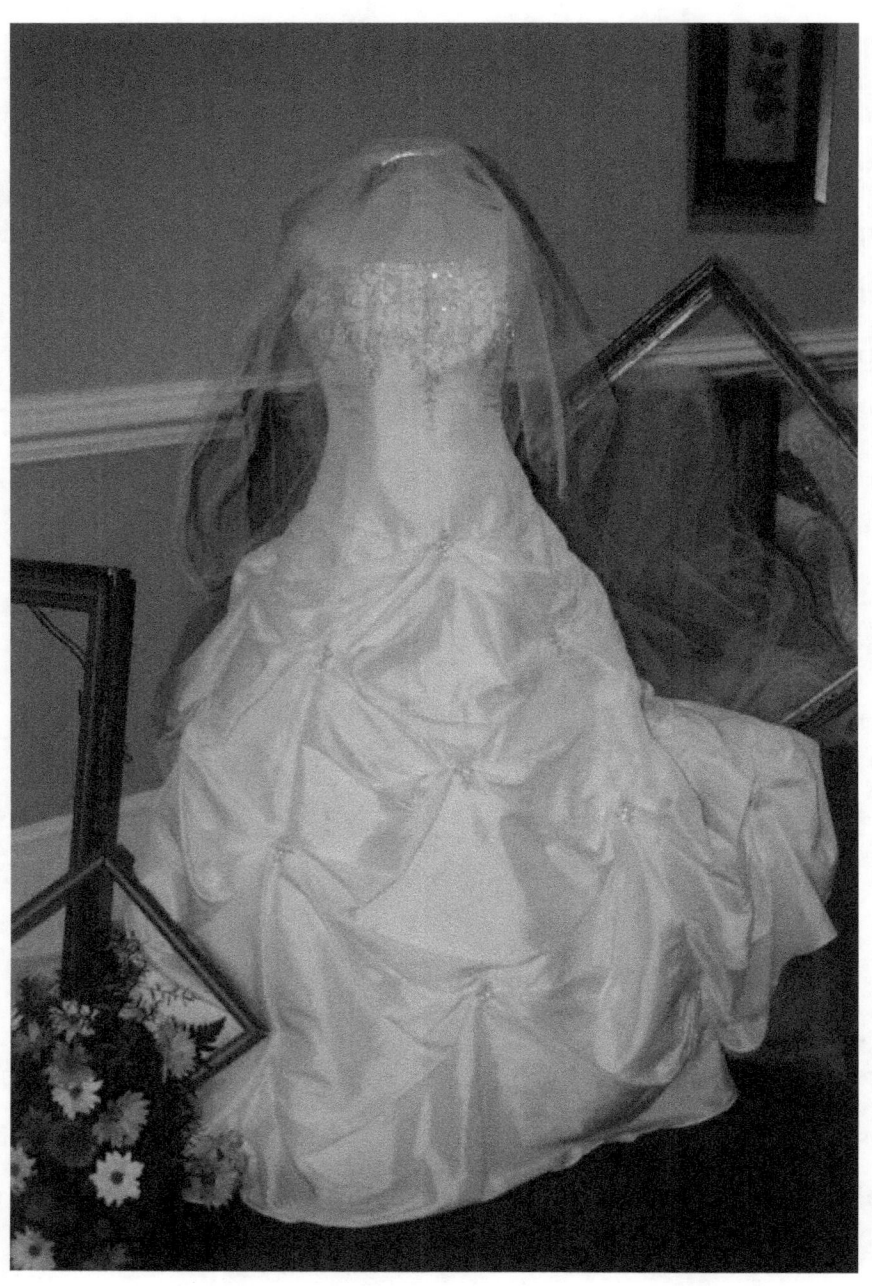

8

Abstract art comes out of the mind of man when he creates something expressing his mood or feelings or anger or frustration or fear or whatever else. God created all the items man uses to express feelings through abstract art.

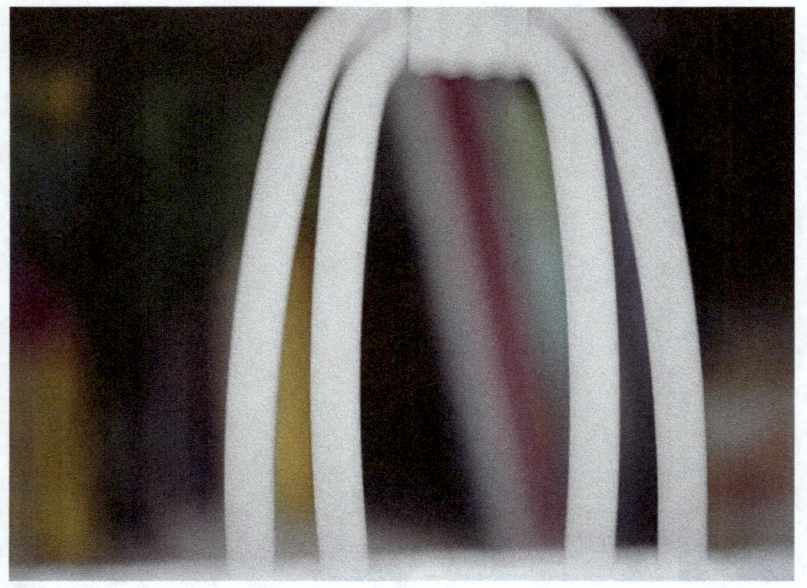

When Paul was perusing the statues created by men in Greece, he saw one labeled "the unknown god". His take on this was: "Being then God's offspring, we ought not to think that the divine being is like gold or silver or stone, an image formed by the art and imagination of man" (Acts 17:29.) The Greeks wrongly supposed they had created something they could worship other than the Lord of the universe. Paul was intent on disproving this.

He wanted Truth to be known to all men/women/children of the world. He was not fooled by a sculpture of an "unknown god" falsely being touted as a god and being falsely worshiped.

Abstract art is interesting in that men express feelings. Attributing a false name or label to it; however, is wrong. Suppose I decided to name my abstract photography with a name of a so-called god. Would that make it God? No. We humans fabricate false gods out of the substances God has provided. We attach value to objects. Our idols are made of leather and fabric (clothes), gold and silver (jewelry), wood and brick (houses), metal (cars), plastic (just about *everything* else). Too often we say we don't make images such as the idols made in Old Testament times; however, this is not true. We do make images out of substances God has provided. Think about the monetary value we place on art or our cars and buildings.

Look at tools man has invented to see the sky, stars, moons, galaxies. God created *all* these. We can only see what our man-made inventions allow. God sees all His created universe. My mind is blown by considering the universe God created. For us. For humankind. "'And beware lest you raise your eyes to heaven, and when you see the sun and the moon and the stars, all the host of heaven, you be drawn away and bow down to them and serve them, things that the LORD your God has allotted to all the peoples under the whole heaven'" (Deuteronomy 4:19). How often have you wished upon a star? God answers our prayers in our best interest. Think about praying to God. Look at the night sky and stars. Remember the One Who *created* the heavens with its numerous stars. And Who surely answers prayers.

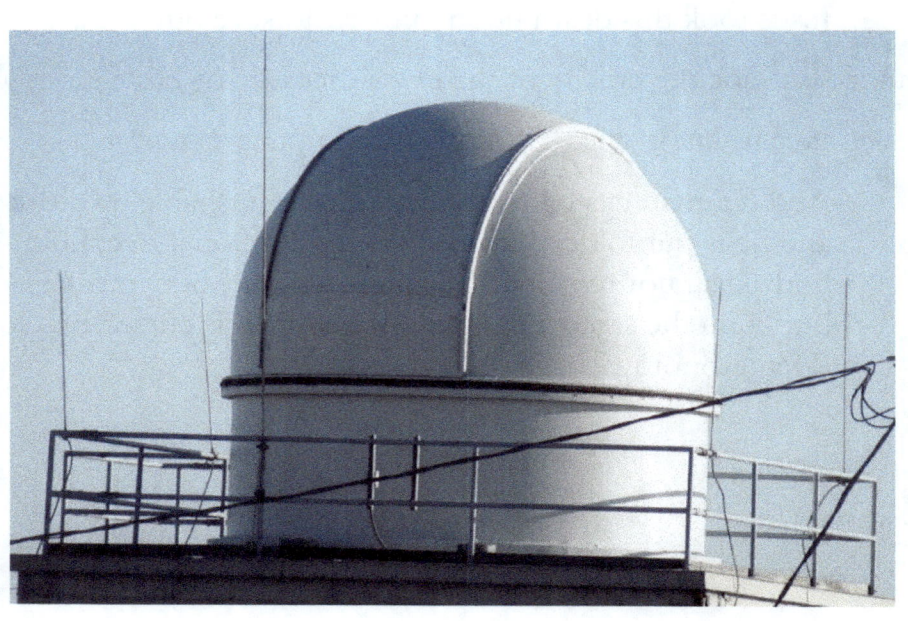

We attend church to worship our Lord. The ultimate cruel man-made object was provided for Jesus' death – a cross. His death provided our lives – for His children anyway.

We can make a cross look so nice and pretty, even hanging a beautiful jewelry piece around our necks. Yet it was a cruel, man-invented and man-made implement of the worst kind of death known to man used to kill our Savior.

Jesus took this death upon Himself to save our lives. We cannot imagine the cruelty of the cross. Because of His action, we never have to know what He suffered upon that *Cross*.

> And if a man has committed a crime punishable by death and he is put to death, and you hang him on a tree, his body shall not remain all night on the tree, but you shall bury him the same day, for a hanged man is cursed by God. (Deuteronomy 21:22-23a)

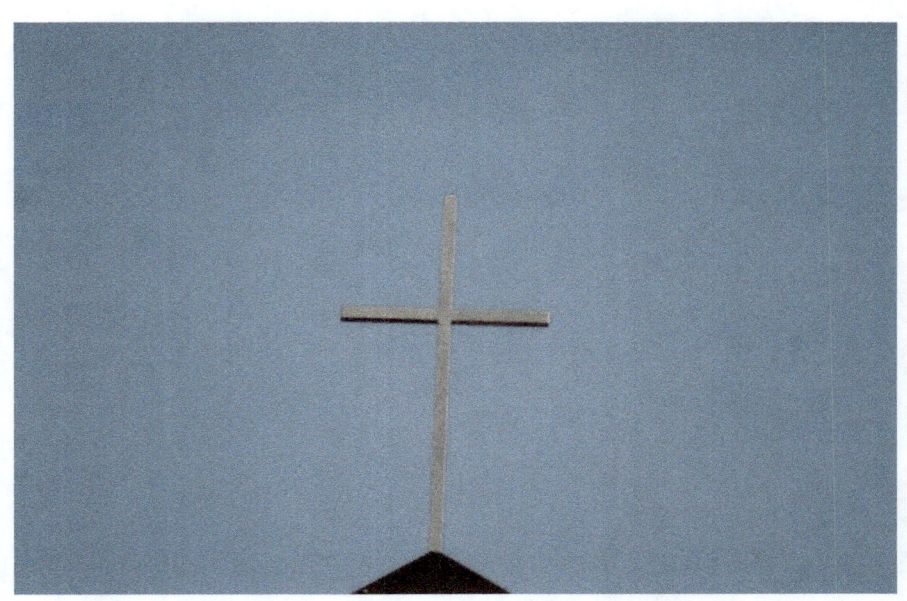

Final Thoughts

We are not cursed because Jesus took *our* curse upon Himself. The above verse speaks of a man committing a horrific crime, punishable by death. The truth is, Jesus committed *no* crime. No crime at all. He was still hung on a cross. The worst man-made invention ever used became the life-giving instrument for *our* salvation.

Man-made inventions, creations, and objects of art are all possible because of the life and death of our Lord and Savior. We can't create *anything* out of nothing. God could only accomplish this seemingly impossible task. We owe it all to Him. *Everything.*

"Not to us, O LORD, not to us, but to your name give glory, for the sake of your steadfast love and your faithfulness! ... The heavens are the LORD's heavens, but the earth he has given to the children of man" (Psalm 115:1, 16).

The truth is man has attempted since the beginning of his existence to create something more satisfying than God. He forgets God is the Creator. Not man. The man-made objects are available simply due to the fact God created the substances from which they are manufactured.

We desperately seek fulfillment on earth outside of God. This tragic fact is how we get into predicaments for which we attempt to extricate ourselves. God, however, still protects us, watches over us, gives us signs and warnings, bells and whistles to warn us of danger, and ultimately provides the ground we walk upon. Without God we are doomed. We cannot outdo Him or create something for which He did not provide the material.

Man insists upon being as much like God as possible. He thinks his inventions will outdo God and provide us the ability to not need God at all. Ecclesiastes is the book speaking most about our attempt to be better and more needed than God. David Gibson wrote about his thoughts on the book of Ecclesiastes and how we attempt our poor effort to outdo God:

> The point [William] Powers makes about the digital age applies to everything under the sun. A new government is still a government, and we're all familiar with those. A revolution heralds a new era, and we've seen it all before. A new baby is still a baby, and the world has always been full of them. Even landing on the moon is still a form of adventure and exploration that has been with us since humans have walked the earth. Indeed, space travel is a good example of precisely the Preacher's point. He doesn't mean no "new" things are ever invented in the world, for clearly that is not true. He means there is nothing new we can ever discover to break the cycle and so satisfy us. When we conquer our solar system, humanity will then try to conquer the galaxy beyond it. We never have our fill, and that basic human impulse that led us to space in the first place "has been already in the age before us" (v. 10). There

is nothing new about humanity in the unfolding of all our progress.[1]

Men "create" man-made objects with eyes and activities facing toward outdoing God's creation. Man too often lives unaware of the necessity of facing *toward* the God of the universe with a thankful heart for all God has provided for man to use to "create".

The next time you pick up a spatula to turn your food over in your pan, on your stove, in your cozy kitchen, place the food on your sturdy, prettily-set table, drive your car, sleep on a bed, purchase the items you need and/or want, remember Who you belong to and Who made it possible for all these things to exist. And Who created our minds to invent and make these items.

I deeply appreciate the God-made substances from which we obtain our man-made objects. It does seem to make life a bit more satisfying at times; however, I do not want to forget from where these come. Our God. Our grand, majestic, magnificent, and ever-loving God is the One Who granted all this to us. Let's take care of God's Creation for Him as long as we are on this unique earth.

---

[1] LIVING LIFE DRAWKCAB, David Gibson, © 2017, Crossway, Wheaton, IL, p. 26

Our God. Our Lord. Our Savior. Praise be to Him! "For from him and through him and to him are all things. To him be glory forever. Amen." (Romans 11:36)

Scripture quoted:

(In order of appearance)

Genesis 1:28
Matthew 28:18-20
Mark 12:30-31
Ezekiel 8:12
Psalm 24
James 5:7
1 Corinthians 3:12-13
Mark 12:1
Luke 7:36-38
Luke 7:48b, 50b
Genesis 14:18-19
Joshua 2:15
1 Samuel 16:23
1 John 5:13
John 21:25
Jeremiah 29:11-12
Hebrews 6:19-20
Hebrews 1:3a
Proverbs 27:19
1 Corinthians 13:12
Leviticus 2:5-8
Revelation 5:8
Deuteronomy 26:4
Job 23:11
1 Corinthians 10:13
John 3:8
Genesis 1:3
John 9:5
1 John 2:8
Revelation 22:5

Psalm 119:105
Genesis 11:4
Revelation 16:19
Matthew 6:26a
Luke 9:57-58
Philippians 1:27-28
Isaiah 40:15
Numbers 24:7
2 Corinthians 4:7
Ezekiel 27:5
Isaiah 44:14-17
Revelation 21:1-2
Job 14:16-17
2 Kings 4:9
2 Kings 4:10
Ephesians 6:14-15
Matthew 3:11
Mark 9:42
Exodus 22:22-23
Isaiah 5:26
Proverbs 22:3, 27:12
Revelation 11:19
Genesis 28:12
2 Corinthians 8:19
Proverbs 31:24
Jeremiah 17:13
John 7:38
Luke 12:24a
Psalm 65:11
2 Kings 18:19c-20
John 10:1-3
Psalm 91:1-2
Psalm 55:6
Isaiah 23:18

John 14:1-4
Matthew 1:20-21
1 Peter 1:25
1 Timothy 3:15b-c
Ecclesiastes 1:6
Job 26:7-10
Revelation 19:6c-8b
Acts 17:29
Deuteronomy 4:19
Deuteronomy 21:22-23a
Psalm 115:1, 16
Romans 11:36

Photographs:
(In order of appearance)

Camera – Colorado
Gate - Oklahoma
Farm machinery – Colorado
Hay bales – Oklahoma
Fence - Colorado
Restaurant table – North Carolina
Bread - Colorado
Rope on dock – Florida
Piano – North Carolina
Typewriter - Colorado
Books in library – North Carolina
Torn Bible – Florida
Anchor – Florida
Footprint in sand – Florida
Reflection in water - Oklahoma
Old stove – Georgia
Bowl – Colorado
Basket - Georgia
Stone steps – Colorado
Windmill – Oklahoma
Lighthouse – Pacific coast
Candle – Florida
Lamp - Washington
Space Needle – Seattle, Washington
Downtown – Seattle, Washington
Birdhouse – North Carolina
Nest inside pole - Washington
Street signs – Georgia
Holy bucket – Georgia
Hands forming clay - Georgia

Ships at sunset – Florida
Old gas pumps – Georgia
Bicycle – Florida
Suitcases – Florida
Chair – Florida
Boot – North Carolina
Sandal – Florida
Millstones – Tennessee
Church bell – Georgia
Red whistle - Colorado
Cart – Georgia
Ladder - Colorado
Old car – Georgia
Train – Georgia
Fountain – Georgia
Barn – Georgia
Railroad tracks – Colorado
Chess board – Colorado
Greenhouse door – Georgia
Covered bridge – Georgia
Hot air balloons – Colorado
Old store - Georgia
Old house- Georgia
Angel – Georgia
Church pulpit – Georgia
White chapel – Colorado
Wheel – Colorado
Glass ball - Georgia
Wedding dress – Florida
Abstract – Colorado
Abstract – Colorado
Observatory – Florida
Cross on church – Georgia

www.ingramcontent.com/pod-product-compliance
Lightning Source LLC
Chambersburg PA
CBHW070233180526
45158CB00001BA/459